Say
Yes
to
Happiness

MIND
BODY
HEART
SPIRIT

A Handbook
for *Life*

JANE SCHREINER

Say Yes to Happiness: A Handbook for Life
Published by Currans Publishing House
Colorado Springs, CO

ISBN: 978-1-7336068-0-6
SELF-HELP / Personal Growth / Happiness

Cover and Interior design by Victoria Wolf
Photography by Jay Billups Creative Media

QUANTITY PURCHASES: Schools, companies, professional groups, clubs, and other organizations may qualify for special terms when ordering quantities of this title. For information, email jane@happiness-is-a-skill.com.

CURRANS
PUBLISHING HOUSE

Dedication

With infinite gratitude, this handbook is dedicated to my children: Frankie, Susie, Sammy, and Ellie, who have been present through all of the learning and striving in discovering that happiness is a skill.

Table of Contents

Part 4 HEART

Part 5 SPIRIT

Part 6 CONCLUSION

Say YES to Happiness

Introduction

It's my experience that the longer you sustain a state of happiness, the more natural it becomes. That's been the "Aha!" for me as I've lived and practiced happiness skills .

You are most likely reading this because you are looking for something in your life to help you feel better. Maybe you're trying to make a choice and feel stuck, uncertain. You may be in pain in a relationship and don't know where to turn. Perhaps you've been searching for happiness—for relief from being unhappy too much of the time. Whatever your particular situation, there are answers for you here.

As books often are, this book was written over a long period of years. I grew and changed and developed these practices through those years, so you may hear different voices of me as you read this. That's exactly the point of this work: to learn and grow and explore who you are. Just as I did.

As a small child, I was aware when I didn't feel good—when I wasn't happy. Children keep life simple: It either feels good or it doesn't. Though I was outwardly warm and outgoing, I struggled with unhappiness, which led me to search for ways to feel better. It sounds like a big undertaking for a child, and it was. That search led me to many answers I am sharing here.

From that time until now, some sixty years later, I have been a student and researcher of happiness. I've set up and lived through "life experiments," experiences of my own making, which means I've learned from painful lessons how to live my way into happiness. The common thread throughout all of these years was actively searching for happiness. First, I searched in the "quick fix no fix" places of food, alcohol, and relationships while turning to multiple therapists, meditation gurus and spiritual teachers, workshops, books, tapes, and retreats. Added in were psychic readings and practices, body work and studies in movement, Buddhist teachings and practices, heart-opening yoga, tai chi, and more. Also included was a dust-off of my childhood religious teachings to find the underpinnings of God that resonate for me still, though those underpinnings didn't involve a church. It's been a very long road, and I now know that living in happiness comes from learning and practicing happiness skills daily. Hence this book.

After a surgery in 2008, I was recovering at home. I was up mopping the kitchen floor because "doing" was my balancing activity whenever control was taken away. There I was in my nightgown, mopping and rolling over in my head all I had learned on the topic of happiness. I was always doing that, processing and allowing things to land that would guide me to my next steps. My kids grew up with Post-it Notes on our cupboards and walls heralding my most recent thoughts and epiphanies and all I was learning.

That day with the mopping, I was pushing that mop back and forth and the words "happiness is a skill" came to me. That was it. I leaned the mop against the wall, went to the Post-it Note pad, and wrote that on a piece of paper, which promptly went up on a kitchen cupboard. I have that note still. It keeps me humble and grounded—in deep appreciation for the many messages that frequently land in my knowing. That ability to "hear" comes with all the practices I teach in this handbook. A clear open heart and mind make all the good stuff possible!

In this handbook you will learn happiness concepts and the skills to practice each concept. For example, you're going to learn that your thoughts impact your happiness, and then you'll learn the skills to make positive thoughts central to your way of thinking.

The handbook is presented in four sections that represent the four aspects of you: your mind, body, heart, and spirit. Throughout this handbook you will notice an overlap of concepts within these four areas. This is how the full circle of your being works, from head identifying tasks, body supporting the good journey, heart imbuing it all with goodness, and spirit being the reservoir of fulfillment.

Though I have separated skills and practices into subtopics for reading purposes, the fact remains that living in happiness takes place on a continuum, as you are a whole being; the basics weave through your behaviors and choices. It's pretty cool, actually . It also means that by going through the whole handbook and committing to learn and practice the skills, you will round into all areas of the continuum over and over, which means your happiness skills will continue to strengthen and provide a brilliant lens for your life. That's the goal!

In my coaching I share with clients that living into the change they want ultimately rests with their commitment to growth, to learning, and to practice, practice and more practicing of the things you are going to learn in this handbook. You'll come to know that taking the best possible care of yourself from a place of loving kindness is the heart of this work. The commitment you make is to yourself and for yourself, and this impacts your whole life and everyone around you. Yes, you can live with happiness, fulfillment, and a sense of value in your every day. Create a good moment and repeat, repeat, repeat!

*I'm holding space for your learning and
practice, so let's go.
Love and light for your happiness,
Jane*

Say YES to Happiness

How to Use this Handbook

This handbook is for you to use as you develop your Happiness Is a Skill practice plan and as an ongoing reference. It is a companion for your personal journey to more happiness.

There are four sections here with five subsections in each. Some are shorter than others and require less time. Some of them will take you more time to complete.

It's so important for you to go at your own pace through this book; it's a process, and a process takes time. Prepare for success by planning where you will do the reading and the exercises in advance. Your office, an easy chair in the living room, maybe at your kitchen table? What will your schedule be? What do you want to have with you when you sit down? Your water bottle, a cup of tea, or coffee? And remember your journal too.

You will need to have a journal you really like for this—one that's easy to write in, to look at, to have around. This is going to be in your life now. You also need several easy writing pens that you enjoy writing with. Pens that can keep up with all you have to say. If you're thinking that you don't have anything to write, trust me; it's there.

Working in this book isn't just about the reading; it's really about learning and practicing the skills as you go along. This will take whatever amount of time you need to study, learn, and practice your new happiness skills. There's no need to be in a hurry.

If you haven't been as happy as you want to be, then change is in order, and that's why you're reading this. As you go through the handbook and choose the things that resonate for you, it's essential that you set yourself up to do the practices consistently. This is why you are directed to

post reminders, visual prompts, and affirmations of the things you want to be thinking about and doing now.

The key to creating change is the sustained repetition of that which is being learned. Hence the concept of practice, over and over, until each happiness skill becomes your normal behavior. In many places throughout the handbook, you will be prompted to remind yourself of new thoughts and of your commitments to try new things. You will be asked to set ways to remind yourself. This matters. There are no short-cuts to change, so settle in and take the time to go through this at your own pace.

This handbook is a serious companion for happiness growth and change. Take the teachings, skills, and practices into your life, commit to use them, follow the guidance, and see how much happier you become.

Here's to being
your happiest self!

Layout

There are nice, wide margins for recording notes about your thoughts and ideas as you go through the handbook. Have fun with those. :)

Next to each skill there is a yellow check box. Put a check mark next to each skill that you want to learn and practice. Check the yellow boxes both in the section and in the summary at the end of the section.

There are nine icons throughout the margins as well. Those icons will bring your attention to the nine happiness practices that are key throughout the process. The icons help to integrate these ideas into your way of thinking.

Learning and practicing each skill that you choose from the handbook brings you closer to your own sustainable happiness.

The nine happiness practices with icons are as follows:

 Journaling

 Breathing

 Observing

 Listening to Yourself and Others

 Moving

 Planning

 Using Post-it Notes

 Setting Phone Reminders

 Using Your Phone Timer

Get these ready before you start the handbook:

A journal that you really like

Two or more pens and pencils you like to write with; it's important to have a backup!

Post-it Notes

Schedule time in your planner for regular handbook time throughout the week or the month; do it now before you begin. Schedule thirty minutes, or maybe an hour, at a time over the next weeks or maybe months. Allow enough time to focus and engage with the process. This is like taking a class on happiness, and it's a great way to use your time.

Journaling

This is a primary practice throughout the handbook, so let's begin by looking more closely at what this is.

The journaling we talk about here is not the "dear diary" of your youth; in other words, it's not just a place to keep track of what happened each day. This is a place to freewrite whatever you're thinking, recording ideas you want to remember. It's a place to make notes about what you want to do next and to look into your feelings. If you prefer to process thoughts and feelings out loud, you can use your phone and take voice notes or make video recordings. Regardless of format, so much more can be accomplished when you have a safe, comfortable place to process.

Whether writing or recording, your journal becomes an important place to review ideas and emotions as you go through the Happiness Is a Skill training. You'll have more clarity and learning, and you'll discover more about yourself this way. The entire process of developing happiness skills is about evolving your relationship with yourself; you are the only person who is always there and will always be there, with you.

With respect to choosing your journal, it can be a spiral from the grocery store with a flower on it or a Moleskine notebook from the bookstore. I had one client who loved decorated, leather-bound journals. I use spiral-bound drawing notebooks without lines so I can write all over the page and open it to lie flat on the table. Whatever journal you love the feel of is the right choice for you. Also get several pens that feel good and easy to write with—"fast writers"—since you are going to want your pens to keep up with your hand!

The fun of journaling is letting go of the outcome of your writing, letting go of thought, and simply putting pen to paper and keeping your hand moving, which can reveal much to you that might otherwise be elusive. I've had many things become clear as I've journaled regularly each day.

It's like building a muscle; it grows stronger with use, and it's a great tool for getting clear about decisions and life direction.

Setting a timer as you journal allows you to let go and write. Set it for ten, fifteen, or twenty minutes as you begin your journaling session. Go longer if you want to. You can write anytime throughout the day. Just try to make it daily; daily practice is best. Also, no editing; keep your hand moving. This is important. What you are writing is only for you, and your heart gets to have its say, unfettered. Shine the light into all of those nooks and crannies, and let whatever you discover flow onto the page. Punctuation is not important!

When you journal, you will get clear on what you're feeling. Your whole self will come to count on having this time each day to clear out what is there. It's a safe place to say it all without responses. Your time, your flow. It's a thought-, feeling-, soul-processing skill.

Author Julia Cameron coined the phrase for a specific form of journaling called Morning Pages. It's a best practice for giving your heart, mind, and soul a voice to provide fresh air to power your new day. In Morning Pages, you set your timer and write each morning as you begin your day, releasing all that may have landed during the night so you are clear for the new day. Just put your hand on the page and write until the timer goes off.

You may also want to jot down things in your journal when you only have a quick minute—things that bother you and make you curious and things you want to give more thought to later when you have time. Then you can come back and write more about those things, airing them out so they don't get stuck in your subconscious. Consider keeping your journal with you for when inspiration strikes.

Embrace journaling. If it feels awkward, uncomfortable, or hard at first, keep going. If you are self-conscious in any way about your writing, for any reason, let that go! Your journal is only for you and is a tool for growing self-love and acceptance. Practice that here. As with all happiness skills, consistency is the key.

In short, journaling is simply a good way of keeping open communication with yourself. After all, open, honest communication that takes place often and regularly is key in maintaining healthy relationships, and you are in a relationship with you. Journaling gives your heart and emotions a place to download all that's present instead of keeping things locked up inside, which causes unhappiness. Unhappiness is not what we're about here. :)

Community

You may want to share ideas and read how other people are doing with their Say Yes to Happiness handbook, and you can do that by going to the Say Yes to the Happiness handbook group on Facebook. It's a private page for group members to support one another, make connections, and share community. Those are some of your heart happiness skills!!

The Quick Reference Guide to Happiness Skills & Practices

The following two pages are a quick-view reference guide for you while going through the book and choosing which skills you'll use. As you go through the book, you may want to practice all the skills or choose only a few things that resonate for you. The key is to practice them daily to create and sustain the changes you want to make.

As you use the check boxes throughout the book, you will be designing what a day in your life will now look like.

For example, you may check boxes for living the roles you love, as you accomplish your goals for that day, setting a timer to meditate and breathe as you go along. Then looking up to energize as you begin a day doing things that serve your values. After that you might connect with people through deep listening with kindness and share your gratitude, ending your day with a few minutes writing in your journal about everything that's on your mind and in your heart. You'll choose what feels good to you and live your way into days filled with more happiness.

Daily practice is the way to make change. The commitment to persist and continuously use your new practices is what will get you where you want to be. If you miss a day or more, simply come back to the skill and continue on practicing. The mantra is to "keep coming back" to that which serves you and feels satisfying and fulfilling.

The quick reference guide and the skills summaries at the end of each section and subsection, are all there for you to keep track of the skills and practices you are saying yes to doing consistently. You can use the Quick Reference Guide as your own master list to live by.

Choose you. Say yes to happiness.
You're worth it.

Quick Reference Guide to

Mind 1
WHAT YOU THINK IS WHAT YOU CREATE

- [ ] *Shifting Your Thoughts*
- [ ] *Change Your Words*
- [ ] *Think 3 Things*
- [ ] *Set Your Phone Timer*
- [ ] *Write Your Personal Support Mantra*
- [ ] *Positive Words and Phrases to See*
- [ ] *Get Daily Affirmation Card Decks*
- [ ] *Hit the Refresh Button*
- [ ] *Humor and Laughter*

Mind 2
KEYS TO CHANGING YOUR THOUGHTS: BELIEF, VISUALIZATION, AND INTENTION

- [ ] *Rewrite Your Limiting Beliefs*
- [ ] *If You Can See It, You Can Make It So*
- [ ] *Write Your Story*
- [ ] *Quick Fixes with Imagination and Visualization*
- [ ] *Powerful Belief Awareness*

Mind 3
SURROUND YOURSELF WITH ALL THE RIGHT THINGS

- [ ] *Choice*
- [ ] *Awareness*
- [ ] *Setting Your Intention*
- [ ] *Using Your Five Senses*
- [ ] *Quick Shifts*

Mind 4
LIVING ON PURPOSE

- [ ] *Clarifying Your Values*
- [ ] *Looking at Your Roles in Life*
- [ ] *Writing Your Purpose Statement*

Mind 5
MOVING FORWARD FEARLESSLY

- [ ] *Goal Setting and Action Steps*
- [ ] *Identify Your Goals*
- [ ] *Write Your Story*
- [ ] *Set Your Intention with a Written Vision Statement*
- [ ] *Schedule the Steps in Your Planner*
- [ ] *Journal About Your Commitment to These Decisions*
- [ ] *Continue to Use This Process for All of Your Goals*

Heart 1
SELF-LOVE

- [ ] *What Do You Value about You?*
- [ ] *Being Your Own Best Friend*
- [ ] *Self-Nurture, Self Care*
- [ ] *Cultivating Self Love*
- [ ] *Connecting with Your Younger Self*
- [ ] *Fun Alone Time with You!*
- [ ] *How Are You Doing Loving Yourself?*

Heart 2
THE POWER OF CONNECTION

- [ ] *Connect!*
- [ ] *Relationship Boundaries*
- [ ] *Observe Yourself*
- [ ] *Journal Your Observations*

Heart 3
GIVING AND RECEIVING

- [ ] *Make a Commitment to Give*
- [ ] *Set Your Intention to Give*
- [ ] *Notice Your Feelings*
- [ ] *Set Your Intention to Receive*
- [ ] *Ask for What You Need*
- [ ] *Saying Yes and Saying No*

Heart 4
GRATITUDE IS AMAZING

- [ ] *Think Grateful Thoughts*
- [ ] *Embody Gratitude*
- [ ] *Write It Down: Your Gratitude Journal*
- [ ] *A to Z*
- [ ] *Grateful for Things Large and Small*
- [ ] *Say It Out Loud*
- [ ] *You*

Heart 5
BEING YOUR BEST SELF

- [ ] *Being Aware of Your Accomplishments*
- [ ] *Being a Deep Listener*
- [ ] *Learning to Be Flexible*
- [ ] *Self-Awareness*

Happiness Skills & Practices

Body 1
THE POWER OF MOVEMENT

- [ ] Moving in Figure Eights
- [ ] Tai Chi, Tai Ji, Qigong, Yoga
- [ ] The Reset
- [ ] Hands to Heart
- [ ] Hands to Stomach
- [ ] Centering
- [ ] Stand Straight, Shoulders Back, Chin up
- [ ] Move!
- [ ] Mountain Pose
- [ ] Lie on the Ground
- [ ] Get in Your Heels
- [ ] Breathe Slowly and Deeply

Body 2
GROUNDING: THE POWER OF STILLNESS

- [ ] Mountain Pose
- [ ] Lie on the Ground
- [ ] Get in Your Heels
- [ ] Breathe Slowly and Deeply

Body 3
BODY VOICES

- [ ] What Is Your Body Telling You?
- [ ] Sweet-Talk Your Body
- [ ] Take Regular Breaks

Body 4
SUPPORTING YOURSELF

- [ ] Touch: For You and for Others
- [ ] Hugs!
- [ ] Breathe!
- [ ] Look up!
- [ ] Smile
- [ ] Drink Water
- [ ] Arms up!

Body 5
YOUR RELATIONSHIP WITH FOOD

- [ ] The Repeating Phrase
- [ ] Write Your Food Mantra
- [ ] Use it often!

Spirit 1
SPIRIT AND INTUITION

- [ ] Meditation
- [ ] Body Voices
- [ ] Journaling

Spirit 2
CONNECTING WITH SPIRIT: MEDITATION, PEACE, AND BALANCE

- [ ] Meditation
- [ ] Creating Resonance for Connecting with Your Spirit

Spirit 3
MINDFULNESS AND PRESENCE

- [ ] Meditation
- [ ] Movement
- [ ] Breathing
- [ ] Settling into the Earth
- [ ] Listening with Presence
- [ ] Pausing for Presence

Spirit 4
SPIRIT IN ACTION: CURIOSITY, CREATIVITY, COURAGE AND PASSION

- [ ] What Lights Your Fire?
- [ ] Your Unattended Longings
- [ ] Write It Down: Your Gratitude Journal
- [ ] A to Z
- [ ] Grateful for Things Large and Small
- [ ] Say It Out Loud
- [ ] You

Spirit 5
SPIRIT NOURISHMENT: EXPANDING, EXPLORING, LEARNING, AND GROWING

- [ ] Ritual

What You Think is What You Create

The basic rule in happiness is this: "What you think is what you create." Each thought you have creates a feeling. It's that simple.

There is, of course, a process to this, and many supporting skills are needed to achieve and maintain positive thought. Starting here will help to keep you focused on the core of happiness.

Each thought you have results in an elechtrochemical response. This is the center of our emotional responses. If our thoughts have positive associations, then the nervous system elevates levels of dopamine and serotonin, which in turn lifts your mood, your outlook, your spirit. If a thought results in a negative feeling, then epinephrine is released into your system, telling you that all is not well. This chemical generates physical responses intended to prepare your body for a problem. You stay on alert for more trouble, perpetuating negative thinking.

Since thoughts are largely made up of words, the words that we choose to say, hear, read, think, or surround ourselves with in our music, TV, and other entertainment choices are key to setting us up for positive thoughts. Again, the words you choose to surround yourself with—to hear, to say, to read, to think—all need to be considered as you move yourself into a happy life. For example, watching or listening to the news produces an infusion of negative words, stories, and thoughts. Many of the songs we hear lament something lost, emotional angst, or worse. TV shows can be the same, filled with drama and difficulty. The point is to choose what you hear and see from this place of awareness. Choose to surround yourself with things that leave you feeling good—not bad, flat, anxious, and so on. Your choices are key in developing your happiness skills.

As you read on and learn the skills for living this happiness concept, remember this: you become what you think, and what you think about, you bring about.

HAPPINESS SKILLS AND PRACTICES

Shifting Your Thoughts

In order to shift your thoughts, practice the following steps:

1. Notice what you are thinking, how you are feeling, and how you are behaving.

2. If you notice something you don't like, pause and take a deep breath in, fully expanding your stomach and chest. Then exhale completely, breathing out whatever you noticed that wasn't feeling good and letting go of the thought. As you breathe out, release any tension in your shoulders, neck, and jaw, and ease any other tension in your body. This is a full body breath.

3. These steps are effective on their own, and they are the first steps in the following practices. Use them as you try the following skills.

Change Your Words

Consider the following example of change:

You are thinking, "My throat is hurting, and I know I will be sick by tomorrow and home in bed. Darn! I have too much going on to be sick."

Now you change the words to this: "My throat is a little off; I'm going to take some vitamin C and natural remedies. I'll be OK for my day tomorrow!"

The next time you notice yourself going to the negative in an unvoiced thought or spoken thought, pause and think about how you can turn that to a positive thought instead. If you are accustomed to being negative, remember that small steps in this change are good. Keep noticing and shifting to more positive words such as "all will be well."

You Choose The Thoughts You Have, So Pick The Good Ones.

Think 3 Things

When you notice yourself in a place of fear or anxiety, or you are simply dwelling in negativity, try these steps:

A. Pause and take a deep, full-body breath.

B. Use your senses to notice three things around you that are pleasant, that you like.

   Some examples could be the sun shining through the window on your face, soft music coming from your car speakers, the smell of coffee coming from the kitchen, the blue sky with white clouds overhead, or the softness of a sweater you're wearing.

   You get the idea. Notice things that feel good to you.

C. Keep your focus on those three things. Notice how your mood changes because your brain shifted into chemically supporting you to feel better! So simple, right?

Set Your Phone Timer

There may be times when we feel compelled to vent or to dwell in the negative. At these times we might not feel that thought shifting is possible.

If you come to a moment like this, set the timer on your phone for five to ten minutes. That's it!

This is your allotted time to spend dwelling and venting and, OK, even ranting!

When the timer goes off, it is time to move forward into a new perspective and shift to positive thinking.

Note: If your "venting process" includes calling someone to share your frustrations, be sure you have the person's permission first. Simply ask at the beginning of the call if that person is OK listening to your negative stuff. It's important to realize that we all impact one another's attitudes, feelings, and energy. As sure as you are in turmoil in that moment, sharing your negativity with someone else places it in that person's consciousness too. You're asking the recipient to take it on; now he or she has to do something with it! So, ask first.

Your Personal Support Mantra

In moments when you need a quick rescue or a quick shift, your personal support mantra is just the thing.

Maybe you have slipped on the ice and are sprawled on the ground. If the words "I'm OK" are the first words to go through your mind as you are falling and as you land, then your positive attitude will stay in place, and whatever outcome you have will be more manageable. Used this way,

"I'm OK" means that no matter what happens, you are going to be OK. You will come out the other side of the experience. Your brain gets the message and sends serotonin to support your emotional well-being.

This can be especially helpful when people around you are unhappy and doing their best to make sure you know it—whether it's in traffic on the highway or at home with the family. When you feel like others are testing your calm, use your personal support mantra and continue repeating it, either out loud or in your mind. Simple, powerful, effective! Use it any-time you feel challenged to stay steady.

Write Your Personal Support Mantra

Choose a series of words, or a phrase, that feels particularly supportive to you.

Some suggestions are:

I'm doing great!

Kindness, patience, empathy.

That went well.

I get to choose how I handle this.

I know this will work

I hand it over to my higher power.

One day at a time.

Everything always gets better.

Do the next right thing.

This too shall pass.

All is well.

I'm OK!

Be creative! Any words that feel supportive to you are the right words for your mantra or mantras. Post those words in places where you will see and read them often, like your mirror, your car dashboard, and your office. With time, thinking your mantra or mantras will become automatic.

Write your PERSONAL SUPPORT MANTRA/MANTRAS HERE

_____

_____

_____

_____

_____

_____

Positive Words and Phrases to See

Seeing a list of positive words and phrases in easy view provides you with an instant quick shift tool and works to change your natural way of thinking as you read them regularly.

Let's start by listing a few words, then you add your own!

love	*upbeat*	*savor*
kindness	*engaged*	*peace*
giving	*committed*	*love*

receiving	*trying*	*effort*
joy	*trust*	*experience*
sharing	*beautiful*	*nourishment*
fulfillment	*value*	*humor*
goodness	*fun*	*playing*
good intention	*caring*	*creating*

Some examples of phrases could be:

Let it be easy

Take the good and leave the rest

All things possible

Now add words and phrases that you like and want to keep in sight. Do this in the spaces provided.

_____

_____

_____

_____

_____

_____

I recommend you make a list to post where you'll see it often. You can use Post-it Notes or index cards—anything that is fun for you. Post your words and phrases on a kitchen cupboard or your bathroom mirror or take a photo and save it to the lock screen of your phone. This allows you to do the following:

- Say these words and phrases out loud and to yourself frequently as you practice shifting and reframing negative thoughts to positive thoughts.

- Recite these words as a sleep aide when you are trying to go to sleep at night or trying to get back to sleep in the middle of the night.

Daily Affirmation Card Decks
POSITIVE THOUGHTS AT YOUR FINGERTIPS

There are also decks of cards you can buy in order to support your positivity and happiness practice. Draw one or more cards a day for affirmations and self-support. This keeps positive thoughts right at your fingertips! Hay House Publishing offers many such collections, including Power Thought Cards and I Can Do It Cards.

Hit the Refresh Button

Making time that is fun and refreshing to you is a super happiness skill. Whether it's going for a drive, hiking, watching a movie, or reading a book, rest and relaxation matter. This works best when it's peaceful and renewing and is often done while alone or with one other person with whom you can be yourself and at ease. This is creating a time for your mind to clear. You will reengage with life with fresh energy and perspective. You will be amazed at the power of this practice. Set aside time in your planner and hit your refresh button.

What is a good refresh for you?
Put your answers here:

_____

_____

_____

_____

_____

_____

_____

Humor and Laughter

Laughing is an easy brain chemistry shifter. Whether you do so by surrounding yourself with funny friends, family members, or a great comedian, get yourself laughing. Several times a week at least!

What makes you laugh? If you already know, then great! If you need to bring some funny into your life, look online for comedy radio stations, comedy TV stations, and comedy downloads for your phone. Whether at home, working out with earbuds, or driving in your car, laughter is a happiness practice.

Summary

The things I commit to doing

Check the yellow box for each Skill and Practice you are saying 'yes' to. ✔

- ☐ *Shifting Your Thoughts*
- ☐ *Change Your Words*
- ☐ *Think 3 Things*
- ☐ *Set Your Phone Timer*
- ☐ *Write Your Personal Support Mantra*
- ☐ *Positive Words and Phrases to See*
- ☐ *Get Daily Affirmation Card Decks*
- ☐ *Hit the Refresh Button*
- ☐ *Humor and Laughter*

Do you want to create reminders for any of these?

Keys to Changing Your Thoughts: Belief, Visualization and Intention

What you believe and how you see things—your perception—determine much about how you feel.

Consider this: If you believe people are inherently good, then you are going to see people through that lens. From this perspective you will have positive feelings about people and make connections more easily. This, in turn, sets you up for more fulfillment and happiness.

In contrast, if you believe that people are inherently untrustworthy, you may feel fear and suspicion around people. Imagine an unkempt-looking man is walking toward you on the sidewalk. Your mind goes into thoughts of being knocked over the head and robbed. As that person approaches, your breath quickens and becomes shallow, your palms sweat, and your heart races. You're sure that you are about to be assaulted! Certainly there's no happiness in such a belief.

These examples are designed to make the concept clear: Your beliefs and perceptions set up your responses and feelings. Now let's add in choice. This is what makes it possible to create happiness from an otherwise dissonant place. When you consciously choose how you look at something and when you examine your beliefs to see how they are impacting your life, you have the power to make changes that lead to more happiness, peace, and ease.

What beliefs and perceptions do you have that you want to change? These beliefs, because they limit your ability to thrive, are called limiting beliefs. We all have certain beliefs about ourselves, other people, and the world we live in. Maybe you have a limiting belief about your height or what you're capable of doing. We also have limiting beliefs about life and the world, such as feeling that unkempt strangers are dangerous.

HAPPINESS SKILLS AND PRACTICES

Rewrite Your Limiting Beliefs

Here's a five-step process for using choice to shift a limiting belief. Let's try it right now. Choose one of your limiting beliefs and write it below here. Then go through the five-step process.

Example

My Limiting Belief is: *"I believe that I am not smart enough to take a writing class at the local college."*

Step 1.

"This comes from years of thinking I am not smart enough for a lot of things! This is an old habit. My Dad used to tell me that I wasn't very smart and shouldn't expect to go far in life."

Step 2.

"I am committing to being happy in my life, which is why I'm reading this handbook! I am going to be happy!!"

Step 3.

"All is well with me! I am smart, and I know that I am OK, whatever I am doing. My personal support mantra is that I'm OK."

Step 4.

"I can *see* myself taking the writing class, sitting in the classroom, and enjoying every moment. I breathe deeply and slowly as I see this in my mind."

Step 5.

"I notice that I am smiling; I'm a little nervous, but I am excited, and this feels great!""

Now try it with one of your own limiting beliefs.

Write your limiting belief here:

_____

_____

_____

Step 1.

Where does your thought come from? An experience you had or something you were taught by your parents? Write your answer.

_____

_____

_____

_____

_____

_____

_____

Step 2.

Commit to living with more peace, ease, and happiness around this topic. Write your commitment here.

_____

_____

_____

_____

_____

_____

Step 3.

Remind yourself that all is well for you around this belief. This is a good place to rewrite your personal support mantra. Put your reminder here.

_____

_____

_____

_____

_____

_____

Step 4.

Breathe deeply as you see yourself with a new belief, and remind yourself that all is well as you visualize this positive outcome. Write your visualization here.

_____

_____

_____

_____

_____

_____

Step 5.

Smile to yourself as you visualize the positive outcome. Write here how you see this.

_____

_____

_____

_____

_____

_____

Use the 5 step process often as you begin this commitment to shifting your beliefs and perspectives.

If You Can See It, You Can Make It So

In this process, you used imagination and visualization as powerful tools for creating what you wanted in your life. You can see this at work in the example of the stranger on the sidewalk. As you imagine and then visualize the stranger's approach from a place of trusting and empowered thoughts, you are practicing your ability to create a sense of well-being by shifting your perspective.

Imagining and visualizing go hand in hand. You see what you are imagining in your mind's eye, and that is visualization.

Now let's add intention to this. Intention is the determination to act in a certain way, the commitment to new ways of thinking about things. It's a powerful happiness skill.

Here's an example.

Let's say when you awaken in the morning you set your intention to go into the office and keep a smile on your face no matter what. You set this intention in your mind by visualizing—by imagining yourself walking in the office smiling as you greet people. Just to be sure to keep yourself on track, take the time to imagine a grumpy office mate griping about something to you. See yourself keeping a soft smile on your face as you listen politely for a short time before explaining that you need to get to work.

Now each day as you get out of bed, you revisit your "smiling in the office" face. This will start to feel natural as you live your way into this happiness skill each morning!

How can you see this working for you? What's going on in your life that would become easier with setting your intention to approach it in a new way, and visualizing the new outcome in advance? Write about this here.

_____

_____

_____

_____

_____

_____

This is how you use intention, visualization, and imagination, to make happy improvements in your life.

Write Your Story

One way of using imagination and visualization is through writing stories. What we believe and how we see things comes from the stories we have told ourselves about specific topics and situations. As with the five-step process and the example of the man on the sidewalk, if I believe that I can never have what I want, or that nothing good ever happens to me, then I am likely to miss the wonderful that comes along. We get very immersed in our beliefs; these beliefs translate into stories, and we can't see past them. Frequently, stories are about what's wrong instead of what's right. Being so occupied with the negative often robs us of the opportunity to see the positive.

This exercise is designed to give you a jump start into seeing the power of perspective. When you want to create a particular outcome, or achieve a specific result, use your imagination and visualize details about where you are, what you see, what you feel, and what you're doing. Describe who is there, the weather, how it looks and smells, and all of the other details that help bring it to life.

Example

If you were to write a story about your life one year from now, it might go like this:

"I awaken every morning to the scent of pine trees coming through my window. My living room is cool year-round as it's shaded by the big pine trees out back. I always dreamed of living on a quiet road in a cozy cottage but didn't see how I could make it happen. Always being a city person, I didn't know that there were areas where I could get such an affordable place and still have access to the things I love in the city.

I spend two days a week working in the quiet at my cozy kitchen table, and I'm energized by the vibrant blue table I sit at, along with the ergonomically designed chairs that make sitting at my computer so comfortable. I smell the fresh coffee brewing all morning and then see the sunlight streaming in the front windows by early afternoon. The other three days, I catch the train from the station only five minutes away and enjoy listening to books in my earbuds during the thirty-minute ride to the city. I get all my steps in those days as I walk to the office and no longer deal with parking expense and driving through rush hour.

I can't believe how happy I am. I wanted these things and wrote them into my story for the Happiness Is a Skill Workshop last year, and that got me on my way to making it happen!"

Now in your journal, write the story of your life one year, three years, and five years from now. Remember, anytime you are facing something that looks hard to you or difficult in any way, rewrite the story with these steps before going into the situation.

Quick Happiness Fixes with Imagination and Visualization

Try these to feel better quickly:

Imagine people smiling at you.

Visualize the places you love to be.

Imagine things you love to see.

Visualize things that make you laugh.

Imagine the endless possibilities you can create in the moment, the day, in your life!

Powerful Belief Awareness

In our culture there are two things we tend to do that have a large impact on our happiness: making assumptions and taking things personally. I think of this as the one-two belief set. It works like this: we assume that because someone does or does not do something, it's because of us.

Assumptions like this are just stories. We have no idea what the reason for a person's choice really is, but we begin to consider all the possible negative reasons, and those reasons become the story we believe.

Let's say you text someone, and that person does not text you back. At first, you're thrown off; it feels awkward, like you aren't important enough to respond to. You take this personally and feel vulnerable, and your imagination starts to run with it!

Now look at it this way. You text someone. That person doesn't text you back. There could be many reasons for this that you simply cannot know. You choose either to try another form of contact, or you move on without giving it a thought. This feels so much better. You aren't distracted by your own assumptions and aren't taking something personally. This is freeing! You stay on your path for your day, without any drama or distraction. That's the feeling of happiness creation in action. No drama equals way more happiness.

Practice

Practice noticing when you begin to go into assumptions and taking things personally. Release yourself from "writing" that story in your head. Simply detach and move on with whatever you can control to create a good outcome for yourself.

The first several times you do this practice, write about it in your journal. Keep it simple, noting the things that stood out in your experience and what you noticed changing or not changing with yourself. Make any notes that you want to remind yourself to do next time. Doing this will help to grow your self-awareness and your practice of making new choices, which are key to your happiness skills.

Check the yellow box for each Skill and Practice you are saying 'yes' to. ✔

☐ *Rewrite Your Limiting Belief*

☐ *If You Can See It You Can Make It So*

☐ *Write Your Story*

☐ *Quick Fixes with Imagination and Visualization*

☐ *Powerful Belief Awareness*

Do you want to create reminders for any of these?

Surround
Yourself
with
All the
Right
Things

It is essential to surround yourself with things, people, and experiences that support you and lift you up.

This is a key skill for living in happiness. In this section we are going to focus on the impact this has on your brain and on the many choices you have in identifying what the "right things" are for you. Making a choice, then a commitment, and then setting your intention to follow through are the drivers that set you up for happiness! How are you doing with all of those?

Understanding the role brain chemistry plays in your happiness is vital to creating a happy life. When you understand that, you'll make choices with the intention of setting yourself up for more happy moments. As the interplay between choice and chemistry becomes clear, it will be easy to use your senses to surround yourself in ways that support more success and good feeling!

Emotion, behavior, and motivation all come from the brain's limbic system. As humans, we can actually key off of one another's emotional states—a phenomenon known as limbic resonance. This resonance comes as an emotional contagion, spreading from one person to another.

Why does this matter? There are two reasons. First, this illustrates how important it is to choose with care the people you are around. For example, when someone walks in the room who is angry and irritable, you will probably pick up on it, and your otherwise happy state will begin to wobble and shift. This leads us to the second reason: Now that you understand this phenomenon, you can be proactive in using other skills to maintain your happy state. This may include choosing to remove yourself from the presence of that person.

To best support yourself and your work in moving toward a happy, fulfilling life, choosing who you spend time with has an indisputable impact on the quality of your life. You may have friends or family members you think it's necessary to see. You may complain about time with these people and yet continue to say yes to being with them.

If you notice this happening, it's time to shift your perspective. Ask yourself this: Is anyone actually benefiting from these tense, difficult, probably painful connections? Are we all caught in old patterns that diminish the quality of life for everyone involved?

It's important here to understand that you can only control you, your choices, and your behavior. Choosing relationships that support you living happily is an important way of being responsible and proactive in your self-care.

Remember, every moment counts!
Create the ones you want!

HAPPINESS SKILLS AND PRACTICES

Your key practices for this section are choice, awareness, and setting intention.

Choice

How often do you make a conscious choice? This is a choice that involves considering the best decision for you in a given situation. Do you buy organic or not? Turn right or left? Answer the phone or let it go to voice mail? It could also be whether to pause and take a breath when you're getting worked up listening to someone or when to say "no" to an invitation that simply feels wrong to you. Like building a muscle, this skill develops and strengthens as you make more choices. Reading this right now is a conscious choice for improving the quality of your life.

Conscious choice is a required happiness skill. For instance, your selections may include choosing to learn, choosing to practice, or choosing to do the many things that you are reading about in this handbook. This all takes your engaged attention every day. Choosing to be good at your happiness skills will improve the quality of your life.

How about some practice?

Practice

Will you write your intention for the rest of this day or evening? If yes, then do it here.

If not, then write about why not. This is the conscious part.

_____

_____

_____

_____

_____

_____

Let's try another one. Is there something you have been putting off that you'd like to do? If so, write it here and choose when you will take action on it. If you're not ready to commit to doing this, write about why you're not. Be clear and open with yourself as you write. This is being fully conscious about your choice.

_____

_____

_____

_____

_____

_____

_____

Remember, choosing the people you spend time with is key to your happiness. These may be people who do not treat you nicely or take too much of your time. Maybe you simply don't have anything in common anymore, and it's time to create some distance in the relationship. Yes, you can change relationships, and it's OK to do so.

Let's make a list of the people you want to change your relationship with and in what way you want to do this.

On the left put the person's name, and on the right put the way you want to change the relationship. This should be something you can control, like saying "no" more often with respect to getting together or telling someone what your boundary is regarding gossip. You might even choose to simply not answer someone's calls anymore. Make the list according to what you want to change and how to make that change in the best way you can.

Name	How to change the relationship
_____	_____
_____	_____
_____	_____
_____	_____
_____	_____
_____	_____
_____	_____

Awareness

Oftentimes we walk through life without much awareness of what we are doing, thinking, or feeling. We may be disconnected from what we believe and what we want. In order to develop happiness skills, you need to grow your awareness of many things. Primarily you will have to become aware of you. Self-awareness is key in noticing what is and is not working for you. Whether it's paying attention to a vague feeling in your gut, the way you are standing and holding your body, or the way you are speaking to someone, pay attention to yourself. Being self-aware empowers you to choose to live with intention in all things that make you happy— all things that fulfill you and bring you that amazing feeling of peace and harmony inside of yourself. Those are happiness skills in action.

Learning to "listen" to your body is a key to self-awareness. Are you clenching your jaw? How are you standing? Are you slumping over with a heaviness that says, "Ugh, I am so unhappy"? Or are you sitting with ease and a smile on your face?

Practice

Below describe everything you notice about your body right now. Some examples may be your posture, any places you notice tight muscles, a feeling of uneasiness in your body, your facial expression, shallow breathing, or a feeling of being cold. Write in detail what you're noticing in this moment.

_____

_____

_____

_____

_____

_____

Being aware of what you feel, what you believe, and what signals your body is sending you in the form of sensations and tightness are all practices you will become good at as you grow your happiness skills.

Let's try another one.

Why are you reading this handbook? Again, go into detail. Include your feelings about why you are reading it.

_____

_____

_____

_____

_____

_____

_____

Setting Your Intention

When you choose to set a specific intention for anything at all, you are actively choosing to create what you want in your life. This is about setting your intention for what you want to be and how you want to be rather than what you want to do. This is not writing a to-do list such as "I intend to make the bed and go to the store today." Intention setting goes deeper into who you are and how you want to be in the day. "Today I intend to be kind, insightful, happy, self-aware." It's fun and powerful.

Practice

Each morning as you awaken, set your intentions for the day. Visualize those intentions. If you've chosen to be kind that day, see yourself doing acts of kindness throughout the day. Visualize yourself fulfilling your intention to manifest it, to make it real. To further set your intentions, write them in your journal or on a Post-it Note to read often as you go through your day. Do this for four weeks and notice what happens. Then keep doing it. These practices are for life!

Examples of intentions for your day could be as follows:

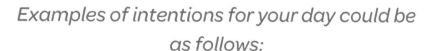

Relationship changes from the list

Self-awareness

Kindness

Learning

Being organized

Patience

Being true to yourself

Honesty

Choices that honor and support you

Being focused

Using Your Five Senses

Stimulating your happy brain through your senses is so easy and effective. Think about how you feel when you look at an amazing sunset or a beautiful work of art. Consider the power of a lovely fragrance to calm and transport you. Perhaps you might choose the softest towels for after your shower and bath because of how nice they feel. Food that tastes incredible can simply change the moment, and listening to your favorite music is uplifting! You can even subscribe to daily uplifting emails to brighten every morning. I'm sure you get the point. When you surround yourself with things that appeal to your senses, you feel happier.

What can you add or change in your daily environment that will feel really good to you? This can be in your car, at your laptop, in rooms and spaces around your home, and in your workplace. Maybe this is adding a photo, loading some music in your phone to listen to, getting a candle or infuser, having your favorite great-tasting healthy snacks close by, or wearing a supersoft sweater. Use your imagination and make a detailed commitment below for setting your senses up to thrive.

I will bring the following things I truly enjoy into my daily environment to

look at.

_____

_____

_____

_____

_____

_____

smell.

_____

_____

_____

_____

_____

touch and feel.

_____

_____

_____

_____

_____

_____

_____

taste.

_____

_____

_____

_____

_____

_____

hear.

_____

_____

_____

_____

_____

_____

 I will do this by _____ (day and date within one week).

Quick Shifts

These are small, quick, and satisfying choices. When you are feeling challenged by something difficult and you notice that you are feeling down or "off," go for a quick walk, jump up and down, smile, dance, or pick one or two quick, fulfilling tasks to do. Maybe it's sending an email, folding the laundry, or cleaning out the passenger seat of your car. Something quick that you have been putting off will reenergize you instantly!

What else can you do to quickly shift yourself into a happier place when you notice you're feeling down or feeling flat? Put a reminder in your phone to remind yourself about quick shifts.

_____

_____

_____

_____

_____

_____

Summary

The things I commit to doing

Check the yellow box for each Skill and Practice you are saying 'yes' to. ✔

☐ *Choice*

☐ *Awareness*

☐ *Setting Your Intention*

☐ *Using Your Five Senses*

☐ *Quick Shifts*

Do you want to create reminders for any of these?

Living
on
Purpose

"I intend to live according to who I am and what's important to me.

By going through this process, I will get in touch with what is deeply true to me and learn how to live in alignment with myself."

Think of a time when you were in the zone—in that sweet spot, fully present, doing something that was so resonant with who you are that you were completely immersed in that moment. Do you have the memory? Can you see it, taste it, hear it? Can you feel the joy of that immersion? That's the happiness that comes from living on purpose, and that sense is a cornerstone of living a fulfilling life.

For many of us, our lives are consumed by things that we think we have to do. We often fall into decisions almost by accident because they feel good or important in the moment, only later to find that we are not happy with those choices. Maybe it's a career that your father said would be a good way to support your family, or perhaps it's the decision to be home raising children because that's what you thought was the "best" choice to make. What's missing from these choices is time taken to identify your sense of purpose. This process invites you to make time to know what you want to dedicate your life to in order to feel resonant with yourself and fulfilled and satisfied at the end of each day. That's powerful, and it's necessary for happiness.

In previous sections we looked at the power of thought in happiness. Now we want to put your focus on what is truly important to you all of the time. This requires you to create a framework to live by that's filled with your sense of purpose and the impact you want to make with your life. In order to get a clear sense of your purpose, you are invited to follow the steps in this section to write your purpose statement. Interested? Good! Get you pens ready, and let's go.

HAPPINESS SKILLS AND PRACTICES

Creating and directing your life from your values, roles, priorities, and personal purpose statement.

Steps in the process:

1. Defining your values

2. Considering the roles you want to fulfill in your life

3. Writing your purpose statement

Clarifying Your Values

The first step is to consider your values. Values ground and guide you—like having all the parts in your life's engine working smoothly together. What are the qualities that you truly want to have guiding your life? What are the most important values for you to live by?

Exercise: Values List

Use the following list for ideas about values and keywords that you choose to live by.

1. Begin by circling the ones that resonate for you.

2. Then come back through and choose up to twelve words as your guiding values.

3. Write each value followed by what's below:

   a. Words that define the value. This is called a "value string," and it will help you clarify each value.

   Here's an example of a value string:

   Let's say you've chosen the value of freedom; your word string could look like this:

   Freedom—travel, choice, no boss, motorcycle, Harley

   In this example you may choose to call this value "Harley." For you the word Harley represents freedom, so you can use Harley in your list! More fun, more meaning. This process should be filled with meaning for you. You're driving toward clarifying your life purpose. It doesn't get any more meaningful than that.

   b. A vision statement.

   Let me start with an example.

   Self-care is one of my highest values, so I wrote this vision statement:

   "I walk under the pine trees for thirty minutes each morning as the sun comes up. I love the movement of walking and the cool pine-scented breeze that get me smiling as this day begins!"

   Here's another one I use for kindness:

   "I smile, nod, and say hi to people I see. I respond with kindness when someone talks to me."

   How about this for being a good listener:

   "I listen from a place of kindness and support, knowing that listening is often all that's needed. I do not offer feedback unless I'm asked, and then I make suggestions rather than tell people what to do."

Vision statements are written in the present tense. This helps you to see yourself living your value right now. Remember, we see it to make it so.

You may actually be living according to many or all of your values already, in which case you can write vision statements that reflect that. An example might be this:

"I go into work each day smiling, calm, and pleasant as I honor my value of bringing goodness to others."

Or perhaps it's this: "I work at the homeless shelter two times a week helping in the kitchen."

Or maybe it's this: "I walk away from the gossip around the office. My value is to stay clear of talking about other people."

These statements give a clear vision of how you live your values, and it's very reinforcing.

Any additional value words beyond the initial twelve can become key words for you and could be included in your purpose statement.

Values and Key Words to Live By

Acceptance	Accomplishment	Accountability
Activeness	Adventure	Affection
Amazement	Appreciation	Approachability
Attentiveness	Awareness	Balance
Beauty	Being a good listener	Being on time
Being your best	Being true to your word	Boldness

Candor	Clarity	Clear focus
Commitment	Community	Compassion
Competence	Completion	Connection
Consciousness	Consistency	Contribution
Cooperation	Courage	Courtesy
Creativity	Curiosity	Delight
Dependability	Depth	Determination
Devotion	Dignity	Directness
Discipline	Discovery	Discretion
Diversity	Drive	Ease
Education	Effectiveness	Elegance
Empathy	Encouragement	Energy
Enthusiasm	Environmentalism	Ethics
Excellence	Experience	Exploration
Expressiveness	Fairness	Faith
Family	Financial Responsibility	Fitness
Flexibility	Flow	Freedom
Friendliness	Friendship	Frugality
Generosity	Giving	Grace
Gratitude	Growth	Happiness
Harmony	Health	Home
Honesty	Honor	Hopefulness
Humility	Humor	Imagination
Impact	Independence	Insightfulness
Inspiration	Integrity	Intimacy
Involvement	Joy	Justice

Kindness	Knowledge	Leadership
Learning	Loving/Love	Loyalty
Making a Difference	Marriage	Mastery
Mindfulness	Open-Mindedness	Partnership
Patience	Passionate living	Peace
Perseverance	Personal Responsibility	Philanthropy
Playfulness	Preparedness	Professionalism
Quiet Time	Receiving	Religious Beliefs
Reflection	Resilience	Respectfulness
Responsibility	Self-Care	Self-Control
Self-Love	Self-Reliance	Self-Respect
Serenity	Service	Sharing
Simplicity	Sincerity	Spirituality
Staying calm	Strength	Structure
Sympathy	Synergy	Thoughtfulness
Tolerance	Transparency	Trust
Trustworthiness	Uniqueness	Usefulness
Vision	Vitality	Volunteering

My list of values, value word strings, and supporting vision statements:

1. Value

_____

Word string

_____

Vision statement

_____

_____

2. Value

_____

Word string

_____

Vision statement

_____

_____

3. Value

_____

Word string

_____

Vision statement

_____

_____

4. Value

_____

Word string

_____

Vision statement

_____

_____

5. Value

_____

Word string

_____

Vision statement

_____

_____

6. Value

_____

Word string

_____

Vision statement

_____

_____

7. Value

_____

Word string

_____

Vision statement

_____

_____

8. Value

_____

Word string

_____

Vision statement

_____

_____

9. Value

_____

Word string

_____

Vision statement

_____

_____

10. Value

_____

Word string

_____

Vision statement

_____

_____

11. Value

_____

Word string

_____

Vision statement

_____

_____

12. Value

_____

Word string

_____

Vision statement

_____

_____

Looking at Your Roles in Life

The second step is identifying the roles that you want to fulfill in your life—roles that are truly the most important for you—and looking at how they can be honored and blended into your life. These may or may not include the roles you already fulfill. You are looking for what feels important inside of you, not what you have chosen from a place of "should."

Exercise: Developing Roles

- List your current roles. Be sure you consider all of your current roles. Think of how you spend your time.

- Consider if you want to continue your current roles. Do they support your values and your sense of purpose, fulfillment, and well-being? Or do they take away from those things? List the roles you no longer want in your life.

- Now consider new roles you want to have in your life. Think of how you want to use your time in a way that you may not be doing now.

- Combine the current list of roles you want to continue with the roles you want to add. List them in order of importance to you. Do not include the roles you no longer want.

Much like with your values, now you will list each role you want and a sentence describing why this role is important to you.

Following are examples of possible roles and a sentence describing what's important about them:

Self

"This role is important to me because the choices I make affect whether I feel good, have energy, and feel powerful! I need all of that to be happy in my life and good at the rest of my roles."

Mother

"Being a mom fills me with my clearest sense of purpose. Talk about a gift."

Daughter

"This role is super important to me, especially now since my dad is alone, having recently lost my mom. It feels really good to be there for him."

As you are thinking of the roles you have in your life, here is a list of possible roles to get you started. Please add your own too!

Father	*Daughter*	*Son*
Wife	*Sibling*	*Coworker*
Friend	*Gardener*	*Musician*
Volunteer	*Student*	

What are your roles?

Current Roles: *Is this a positive or negative for me?*

Do I keep it or let it go?

_____   _____

_____   _____

_____   _____

_____   _____

_____   _____

_____   _____

_____   _____

_____   _____

_____   _____

_____   _____

Roles I would like to add to my life:

_____

_____

_____

_____

_____

_____

My prioritized list of roles I choose
to live and why:

Role:

_____

Describe why this is important.

_____

_____

_____

Role:

_____

Describe why this is important.

_____

_____

_____

Role:

_____

Describe why this is important.

_____

_____

_____

Role:

_____

Describe why this is important.

_____

_____

_____

Role:

_____

Describe why this is important.

_____

_____

_____

Role:

_____

Describe why this is important.

_____

_____

_____

Role:

_____

Describe why this is important.

_____

_____

_____

Role:

_____

Describe why this is important.

_____

_____

_____

Role:

_____

Describe why this is important.

_____

_____

_____

Role:

_____

Describe why this is important.

_____

_____

_____

Writing Your Purpose Statement

A purpose statement is your "why." It reflects why you are here on the planet, what you want to contribute, and the meaning you want your life to have. This is a statement that guides you in living your life and fulfilling your sense of purpose. A purpose statement directs you to live according to your passion and that which nourishes your soul. You live with a sense of accomplishment and happiness when you live according to a well-thought-out purpose statement.

Remember that a purpose statement will be true for you now but will change as you change. This is something you will look at and refine many times in your life. There is no getting it "right." Simply write this from where you are now.

Exercise

Choose several or all of the following questions to answer. Be complete in your answer. This may take time and plenty of paper. If so, allow for that. You want depth and detail. You will consider these answers along with your values and roles when you write the purpose statement that reflects who you are now. This is part of looking at your natural qualities and aligning those with your values and roles as you consider your purpose.

I am at my best when _____.

As a kid, what did I love to do? In school? Extracurricular activities?

What do I really love to do in my personal life?

Name three people I admire and why.

What is the little voice inside of me saying that I haven't taken time to listen to?

If I knew I would succeed, what would I choose to do?

What is the contribution I want to make to the most important people in my life?

My unique contribution to my family, my community, and my work is _____.

What is the impact I want to have at home, in my community, and in the world?

What difference do I want to make with my life?

What is the hunger I can feed, the pain I can ease, the teaching I am called to do?

What is the building I have the tools to accomplish?

It's my one hundredth birthday party, and a tribute is being read about me. What do I want that tribute to say?

At that same party, a young person asks me, "What has your life been for?" What do I want to be able to say to that?

If I had a big, white, digital billboard in Times Square and could put anything on it that I wanted to, what would that be? It could be words, images, or colors, and they could change often since the billboard is digital.

If I had a captive audience of two thousand people and the stage all to myself, what would I want to say to them?

Now, let's write your purpose statement.

"Everything you do, each choice you make, is guided by your purpose statement."

You may write this in one sitting or continue to fine-tune this over time. Either way, as you grow and change, your purpose statement will too. Again, this is a good exercise to revisit every year or so.

1. Let's look at what you've done so far and highlight or circle key words and phrases that you might want to include in your purpose statement.

    a. Do this with your list of values and supporting vision statements.

b. Do this with your prioritized roles and descriptions.

c. Do this with the answers to the above questions.

2. Let the words and phrases you've highlighted guide you in bringing your purpose statement to life. You will have identified many things that are important, and that's good. Your purpose statement can address many things! There is no guideline on length. Simply brainstorm as you begin, remembering that this can be a rough draft or a final copy.

3. Use the space provided to write your statement. You may want to begin at your laptop or on scratch paper, saving this space for your final copy. If you have trouble getting started, try bringing everything you have highlighted onto one sheet or page. You can put them in a list, all over the page in a collage, or in a word map. This gives you a visual tool.

Your completed purpose statement can give you clear direction in making choices that are in alignment with your sense of purpose, who you are, and what you want. That's a powerful tool! Living a resonant life begins with living "on purpose." If you find you're feeling off track in your life, if dissonance has crept in and you are agitated, go to your purpose statement. You'll find that somewhere in your life you're not living in alignment with what you wrote in the statement.

In order for you to integrate this purpose-centered way of being into your life, it's important to keep your statement at the top of your mind. You can memorize it to the tune of a favorite song or put printouts in places where you will frequently see them, including on the desktop of your computer screen or posted on the refrigerator. Some people set a reminder in their phone to pop up periodically. Where is a good place for you to have your purpose statement for easy access and viewing?

Sample Purpose Statements

I believe in living each day to the fullest.

I believe in treating others with the same respect that I myself deserve.

I want to build healthy relationships with others in which we can become one another's biggest advocates.

I will grow stronger with each accomplishment and even stronger with each setback.

I believe everything happens for a reason, and there is no better place to be than right here, right now.

I will not blame others.

I believe in a higher power, and I will let that higher power guide me whenever possible.

To forgive but not forget, so as to learn from each experience.

To find my inner strength and overcome obstacles that hide my goals.

To be guided by my values and beliefs.

To give thanks in some measurable way each day.

To laugh every day.

To act as if I have nothing to lose because, in reality, there truly is nothing to lose.

To show compassion for others in need.

To remember where I have been and where I will go, as I maintain positive relationships with family and friends.

To choose the ethical way by making a personal commitment to honesty and integrity.

To find peacefulness within myself by looking inward while letting my heart guide my dreams and desires and letting my mind pursue knowledge, creating balance among all of my obligations.

To be content in my surroundings, secure with myself wherever I am.

To build a reputation of being dedicated to every goal I choose to pursue while having successes in both my personal and professional life.

To enjoy every moment along this journey—finding laughter, love, and happiness with each day that passes.

My Purpose Statement

_____

_____

_____

_____

_____

_____

_____

_____

_____

_____

_____

Summary

The things I commit to doing

Check the yellow box for each Skill and Practice you are saying 'yes' to. ✔

☐ *Clarifying Your Values*

☐ *Looking at Your Roles in Life*

☐ *Writing Your Purpose Statement*

Do you want to create reminders for any of these?

Moving
Forward
Fearlessly

You know the energy you get when you're in "the zone"?

Time flies by, and you feel amazing. You're humming along doing something that is so in sync with you. This is how it's going to be now that you have the clarity of your purpose statement. Would you like to activate that fulfilling energy every day? That's what you get when you set and achieve your goals, the goals that lead you to living on purpose.

Picture this. You're sitting with your laptop, fingers flying over your keyboard, as the diesel engine repair manual you've dreamed of writing hits the pages. Your purpose led you here, which is to teach people how to repair diesel engines. You're delirious with excitement because you've also landed a job teaching Engines 101 at the community college, which came right out of your vision statement. Bam! You're on purpose! You've set goals, and you're taking steps to achieve them.

Goals set you up to fulfill your purpose in tangible ways. It feels so good when you start with a vision and make that vision your reality. Let's say your purpose is to help young people by teaching. Perhaps your original career was accounting, which you chose because you read that accountants make good money. You've been doing that for several years now, and you're not happy. Then you do the Living on Purpose exercise and have an epiphany that being a teacher working with teenagers is what excites you. You take the leap and change your lifestyle in ways that seem challenging and scary, but you're committed! You go through the doubts, fears, and uncertainties because you can see yourself in that classroom, and you feel the satisfaction of working with those young minds. You get your teaching certificate and a job at a great high school.

The vision and purpose sustained you, and you're there. You had to see it to make it so.

Along with pursuing goals to support your purpose, it's necessary to look at how managing time makes those goals happen. It's like this: If you spend a few minutes on text messages, a few more on Facebook posts, and, oh yeah, Instagram dings, taking you to a bunch of posts there, what happens? Well, you may have fun with a quick zap of distraction but, gosh, the goal you had that was super important to you didn't happen. You only had thirty precious minutes, and those are gone. Now the next really cool thing you were going to do can't happen because you haven't done the first thing.

Time is a most precious commodity. Let me say this again: Time is a most precious commodity. How you use your time is how you use your most valuable resource, which is you! You are the one who is going to live on purpose, achieving awesome purpose-driven goals and living in fulfillment and amazingness. That means using your time for the most valuable things first, foremost, and always.

HAPPINESS SKILLS AND PRACTICES

Goal Setting and Action Steps

The process looks like this:

1. Identify your goals

based on the work you have done naming your values and roles and writing your purpose statement.

Goal: Be a Professional Pilot

2. Set your intention

to achieve those goals. Setting intention always includes visualizing you doing, being, and thinking as if you are already there. Write a vision statement for each goal. Let's write one for this example.

"I fly a really cool private jet for a large corporation. I can see myself in black slacks and shirt as I walk toward the beautiful white plane with blue wing tips waiting in the hangar. I smell the new leather in the plane as I open the door to get in and do the preflight check. Once in the air, I feel the sun on my face as I fly high in the sky and look way down on the ground below. I feel the thrill in my stomach and the warmth in my heart. I love this work."

Goal 1:

_____

Vision Statement:

_____

_____

Goal 2:

_____

Vision Statement:

_____

_____

Goal 3:

_____

Vision Statement:

_____

_____

Goal 4:

_____

Vision Statement:

_____

_____

Goal 5:

_____

Vision Statement:

_____

_____

Goal 6:

_____

Vision Statement:

_____

_____

Goal 7:

_____

Vision Statement:

_____

_____

Goal 8:

_____

Vision Statement:

_____

_____

3. Action steps

are next to make your goal a reality. In this step, you take one goal and write the action steps required to make it happen based on what you know at the time. Action steps may change as you get into the process, and that's OK. You will be writing and rewriting this list as you go along.

Let's continue with the goal of being a professional pilot.

The next step is to write action steps to get you there.

Action Steps to Achieve Goal

A. Research flight schools and degrees for professional pilots and complete it two weeks from now.

B. Research the cost of getting the education and experience to become a professional pilot and complete it two weeks from now.

C. Choose the course of action based on that research within one month.

D. Put funding in place to finance the education within one month of the decision.

E. Apply to a school at the same time.

F. Complete the education in three years.

G. During schooling, learn everything possible about the best resources for getting a flying job.

You get the idea. Write out your action steps with completion dates that will take you step-by-step to achieving your goal.

4. Schedule the steps

you have identified so far in your planner. You will make your best guess about how long each step will take. With practice you'll get really good at planning how much time is needed.

5. Decide that you are going to take each step

needed to accomplish the goal. Write about your decision in your journal. Say it out loud to yourself, and then write it exactly like that in your journal. This may sound obvious, and yet it's a key piece to setting yourself solidly in motion. Your clear decision creates commitment, which is the compass that keeps you on course. This process is about being proactive and deeply committed every day as you move toward your purpose. You have made a series of choices with the clear intention of living a life that resonates for you! Now let's go!

6. Continue this process

as new goals come up for you. Make using your planner for action steps a daily happiness skill.

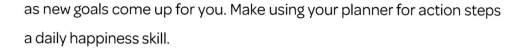

Summary

The things
I commit
to doing

Check the yellow box for each Skill and Practice you are saying 'yes' to. ✔

Goal Setting and Action Steps

☐ *Identify Your Goals*

☐ *Set Your Intention with a Written Vision Statement*

☐ *Plan Your Action Steps*

☐ *Schedule the Steps in Your Planner*

☐ *Journal about Your Commitment to These Decisions*

☐ *Continue to Use This Process for All of Your goals*

Do you want to create reminders for any of these?

Mind

Happiness

Skills

Summary

Would you like to highlight the ones you are saying yes to?

WHAT YOU THINK IS WHAT YOU CREATE

Shifting Your Thoughts

Change Your Words

Think 3 Things

Set Your Phone Timer

Write Your Personal Support Mantra

Positive Words and Phrases to See

Get Daily Affirmation Card Decks

Hit the Refresh Button

Humor and Laughter

KEYS TO CHANGING YOUR THOUGHTS: BELIEF, VISUALIZATION, AND INTENTION

Rewrite Your Limiting Beliefs

If You Can See It, You Can Make It So

Write Your Story

Quick Fixes with Imagination and Visualization

Powerful Belief Awareness

SURROUND YOURSELF WITH
ALL THE RIGHT THINGS

Choice

Awareness

Setting Your Intention

Using Your Five Senses

Quick Shifts

LIVING ON PURPOSE

Clarifying Your Values

Looking at Your Roles in Life

Writing Your Purpose Statement

MOVING FORWARD
FEARLESSLY

Goal Setting and Action Steps

Identify Your Goals

Set Your Intention with a Written Vision Statement

Plan Your Action Steps

Schedule the Steps in Your Planner

Journal About Your Commitment to These Decisions

Continue to Use This Process for All of Your Goals

*Energized! Balanced! Ready to go!
These are expressions that you've probably
used and certainly heard.*

They refer to the connection between your body and how you experience life. Movement is the common thread between them all, and it's a powerful part of you being able to live all of the happiness that's possible for you. As you'll read here, movement helps to release unpleasant feelings and restore you to feeling good.

Think of a time when you were sitting still for too long and needed to stretch your legs. You know that feeling when you get fidgety and need to move. Or how about the opposite—when you've had the best workout, pushing yourself hard and working up a sweat.

In the first scenario, movement was missing, as were the positive chemical messages that are sent to your brain with it. In the second scenario, you flooded your brain with endorphins and were rewarded with the amazingness of high energy and a great feeling.

Movement is a magic reset that you control and can choose any time and any place. Even if you're sitting captive in an airplane seat, you can pedal your legs, rotate your ankles, and sit forward and back. Any movement activates energy and provides relief.

Let me share a story with you. I had a client we will call Sally. Sally was in deep mourning and had to fly cross-country, making several airline connections on her way home from a difficult loss. As she had little to do waiting in the airports between flights, she found grief overtaking her. She started to freeze up, wanting to curl up and drift off to the relief of numbness. Knowing she had to get through this, she stayed on her feet and did something we had worked on together: walking in figure eights. She had her small rolling suitcase, and between the two of them, she and her suitcase, they walked through hundreds of figure eights that day, through two airports, before she made it home. This is what the power of movement and flow looks like in action.

Have you noticed times when simply getting on your feet and moving seemed to make something more manageable? Maybe you noticed it when you were bored, tired, numb with grief, or otherwise feeling unclear. Whenever it's needed, movement will literally move you into feeling better.

Let's look at the ways you can practice this happiness skill in your daily life.

HAPPINESS SKILLS AND PRACTICES

Figure Eights

Figure eights are a pattern for continual motion intended to create a feeling of ease and centering. There is no beginning and no end to a figure eight. The symbol itself stands for wholeness and completion; the continual movement along this pattern offers healing and a sense of calm. It's a dance between your body's motion and your brain's processes that provides this sense of well-being and manageability.

Let's try it right now.

Stand in an open place and visualize being at the center of your figure eight. Now step up and toward the left into the top loop. Continue the shape from there. Do this at least three times, more if you have the time. As in the story of Sally, this can go on as long as it's helpful to you.

Walk it, draw it, and move your body through it.

Moving through the shape of the figure eight can be accomplished in many different ways.

- Walking the shape.

- Standing with your hands outstretched and drawing the shape in the air.

- Adding in whole-body movement as you draw figure eights in the air.

- Drawing the shape by moving your eyes. Talk about activating your brain!

- Doodling the shape everywhere! On paper, in your notebook, and on your walls!

You're naturally creative, so how do you want to create your figure eights?

Tai Chi, Tai Ji, Qigong, Yoga

Simply put, Qigong and Tai Chi, also known as Tai Ji, and yoga strengthen the natural flow of your inner energies and life force, or chi. So it follows that strengthening that which energizes you will bring you a sense of well-being to support your happiness.

Look for classes in your area for any of these practices. These are ancient movements designed to help you thrive. Now those are happiness skills to learn and practice!

The Reset

The Reset is a two-minute practice combining slow, deep breaths and the release of trigger points such as your jaw, tongue, mouth area, shoulders, stomach, hips, knees, ankles, and so on.

Stand with your feet placed evenly, shoulder-width apart.

With a deep breath in, lift your hands up high.

With your exhale, bring your hands back to your sides.

Roll your shoulders up and back.

Settling your shoulder blades down into your back,

Soften your jaw.

Release any tension around your mouth.

Now drop your shoulders.

Breathe deeply in and exhale out while you release any tension in

your stomach. Notice what's there and let it go.

Sway softly side to side as you loosen your hips, and your legs.

Breathe in deeply and exhale fully as you soften your knees.

Allow the tension to run out through the soles of your feet into the floor.

Hold this position for several breaths.

Check your jaw, your shoulders, your stomach.

Let them be at ease.

Now,

bend down to "scoop the earth," with your hands coming together toward each other and bringing that earth energy up with your hands, through your center, your core, and out through the top of your head to connect with the heavens.

As you hold that position, arms extended up toward the sky, visualize yourself as an energy conduit for earth energy coursing up through you into the heavens and then the transfer of that energy going back through you into the earth.

Doing The Reset will ground you when you feel scattered, and it will bring balance and help you to recenter any time you need it.

Hands to Heart

This is an exercise intended to provide support, warmth, and comfort when you are feeling challenged, vulnerable, or otherwise in need of support.

There are two ways to bring energy and balance immediately to your heart with your hands.

As you breathe in deeply, do these things:

- Standing with your weight evenly distributed and feet shoulder-width apart, place your hands, palms flat, one over the other, over your heart. Breathe into your hands.

- You can also do this as you place your hands in prayer position in front of your chest and extend your thumbs back to touch your chest. Breathe in deeply and exhale completely three times.

This will bring ease and the flow of energy around your heart and your chest. Focus on that intention, and your breathing will become easier.

Hands to Stomach

Difficult emotions and situations will often show up as discomfort or uneasiness in our stomachs. To provide support, comfort, and release to your stomach, try this.

- Put your flat palms, with your fingers pointed toward the center of your body, one on top of the other, gently on your stomach.

- Breathe into your hands, holding a slight pressure on your stomach. The idea is for your stomach to feel supported and therefore more at ease. Breathe in and out three times, and do the same again, as much as needed.

You may be a person who experiences stomach dis-ease—stomach discomfort that arises from anxiety that can impact this area. Hands-to-stomach is designed to provide immediate relief to the stomach as needed. This practice can also become an automatic movement with your hands, providing ongoing ease and support. With this, your stomach can experience relief from emotional discomforts that chronically register there.

Centering

This exercise is great when you feel out of balance or out of "whack." Perhaps you're tense and agitated. Try this to bring yourself back to the feeling of being centered.

- Stand square in your feet with your back straight and shoulders lifted and back.

- Flex your knees so you feel anchored to the ground through your feet.

- Place your feet shoulder-width apart, hands hanging loosely at your sides. Shake your shoulders around and loosen them up.

- Now focus first on your in-breath and then your out-breath.

- Relax your trigger points, such as jaw, shoulders, stomach, and hips; put flex in your knees.

- Next, at a moderate pace, lift your arms out to your sides and extend them up to the heavens, palms facing each other.

- Then turn your palms out and bring them back to your sides. Breathe in as you go up, breathe out as you bring your arms down.

- Repeat this movement at least three times, slow and easy. Do it more times if you like. It feels good!

- The last part of this exercise is stopping, closing your eyes, and feeling how centered you are in the core of your body. Notice how solid and anchored you feel in your evenly spaced feet.

- Check your trigger points for being at ease, and feel your connection with the earth, up through your feet, in the breath in your chest, and up through the top of your head.

- Finish by taking your hands to heart and breathing in there. Pause here to notice how solid you feel in the core of your body.

Stand Straight, Shoulders Back and Chin up

Did your mother used to tell you to do this? Mine did. Little did I know how much it does to increase happiness! The messages to the brain with this posture say, "I'm OK. I've got this. All is well!"

Quick, easy, simple! Nice.

Move!

It's really that simple. If your energy is low—or if you are sad, anxious, confused, tired, overwhelmed, or in any difficult situation—then get on your feet and move. Walk, run, dance, jump, wiggle, shake, move!

It's such a gift and great for quick relief.

If you can't stand, then move as you sit or recline. Be creative. You get the idea.

Summary ···

The things
I commit
to doing

Check the yellow box for each Skill and Practice you are saying 'yes' to. ✔

☐ *Moving in Figure Eights*

☐ *Tai Chi, Tai Ji, Qigong, Yoga*

☐ *The Reset*

☐ *Hands to Heart*

☐ *Hands to Stomach*

☐ *Centering*

☐ *Stand Straight, Shoulders Back, Chin up*

☐ *Move!*

Do you want to create reminders for any of these?

Grounding: The Power of Stillness

I have a real problem with stillness. With just stopping and being quiet.

—Gillian Anderson

Does Gillian sound like you? If so, you are not alone. We have created a world of doing and overdoing. The incessant stimulation of digital media is rather like a continuous knocking at the door, relentlessly tugging at our attention. So, yes, being quiet can be a real challenge and even frightening to some people.

It's OK; you can change this.

"Why would I," you ask?

Because you aren't as happy as you'd like to be, which is why you are reading this handbook.

No matter what we have created and injected into our culture, the human being stays the same. Being grounded and being still are nourishing, nurturing forces in our lives. Our heart being, our mind being, our soul being, our physical being, our human being.

Think of a time when you watched a sunrise or sunset. Do you remember the quiet? The simple peace in the stillness? Perhaps you sat watching the waves come in along the beach or stood quietly outside feeling a breeze on your face. It was a moment of stillness, and you were left with a sense of ease. You were connected to the calm; you were grounded.

In the ease is nourishment for your happiness.
It's that simple.

*Learning how to be still, to really be still
and let life happen—that stillness
becomes a radiance.*

—Morgan Freeman

HAPPINESS SKILLS AND PRACTICES

Mountain Pose

If you are a yoga practitioner, you are already familiar with Mountain Pose. Standing with your feet shoulder-width apart, toes pointed forward, and feet parallel, evenly distribute your weight between your feet.

Rock back and forth a little on your feet, settling into the center of each foot. Flex your knees a little and simply drop into this pose, letting yourself release into the earth. With knees and hips released, bounce a little up and down as you settle into your feet comfortably. Now, as you are still, notice what you feel.

You are supported here. Close your eyes if you like, and be in this stillness for sixty seconds, breathing slowly, deeply. Go longer if you wish! Enjoy this place.

The point is to ground yourself as you are balanced on your feet, simply standing in Mountain Pose. In doing this, you notice the power of simplicity.

Lie on the Ground

Yep, that's all there is to it, just lie down on the ground. The idea is to connect with mother earth and drop yourself into her supportive embrace, letting the earth hold you. It's a feeling of being totally supported and, yes, grounded!

I recommend that you lie on your back, arms outstretched. You may want to put down a towel or something under you, and lying right on the ground is great too. This works on any surface, including concrete or on the floor at home. Use your imagination to feel the support and sense of being held, close your eyes, and completely relax. This is incredibly cathartic!

Do this any time you feel the need to renew. Support yourself and check out for a few minutes. It's a wonderful grounding practice.

Get in Your Heels

Have you ever thought, "I need to slow down; I'm getting ahead of myself." This can happen as you go through your day or when you are in conversation with someone. In these moments, notice your posture. Chances are you are leaning forward with your weight forward on the balls of your feet.

To change your speed, slow down, come into your center, and simply drop your weight onto your heels. Try it right now. Stand up, lean forward like you are going to take a step in a hurry. Notice your weight is forward on the balls of your feet. Now bring your feet parallel with each other and drop your weight back and onto your heels. It's a subtle shift and very grounding.

This is similar to keeping your heels down in your stirrups when you are riding a horse. It helps to keep your seat solidly in the saddle. You are centered, in control, and stable in your life.

This is a great quick fix that you can use anytime, and no one need ever notice. Maybe you're walking into a meeting, feeling a little anxious, and perhaps hurrying. As you walk, simply slow your pace and begin each step with a solidly planted heel. Push off from there, rolling onto the ball of your foot. Try it. Works like a charm!

Breathe Slowly and Deeply

This lesson bears repeating as we go along since the power of breathing fits into so many lessons. When you are being still and grounding your-self, breathing is the foundation that supports you.

Breathe deeply, fully expanding your sides and your stomach, and then fully exhale, pushing the air completely out of your lungs by squeezing your core muscles. Now that's breathing! It's also a simple practice when you want to come to stillness and ground yourself.

Summary

The things I commit to doing

Check the yellow box for each Skill and Practice you are saying 'yes' to. ☑

Mountain Pose

Lie on the Ground

Get in Your Heels

Breathe Slowly and Deeply

Do you want to create reminders for any of these?

There is wisdom in our bodies.

What do I mean by that?

When you have a stomachache, a backache, or a neckache, you can often point directly to something going on in your life that's "a pain in the neck," making you "sick to your stomach." Or you might note something that is "breaking your back." Our bodies are the conduits of all emotions that we experience. They store the good, the bad, and everything in between. This can show up as pain, illness, or other physical sensations.

When you're nervous, your stomach gets queasy. You may notice tingly sensations in your body when you're excited. You can "feel numb" with grief and sadness. These are all examples of the direct impact your emotions have on your physical well-being. As your emotions are directly attached to the thoughts you sustain and the words you say and hear, which we learned in the mind section, you see how these things manifest physically.

I call this phenomenon "body voices." As you practice noticing the "language" of your body, your body's wisdom will help you see when there is something that needs your attention. The trick is to pay attention. Working to heal the pain in your heart, mind, and soul will help to resolve the pain in your body too. They all work together.

HAPPINESS SKILLS AND PRACTICES

What Is Your Body Telling You?

In the section on spirit, you will be reading more about meditation, which is simply quieting your mind. But we can try a little meditative exercise here first.

For this exercise, sit comfortably, breathe deeply, and get quiet in mind and body. Breathe slowly and deeply, in and out completely three times. Now ask your body, "What is causing you to hurt?"

Be slow. Allow time after you've asked the question. You may have several thoughts come up. Don't attach to any of them; just notice and listen.

Trust the things that pop into your mind. You may get a picture of your boss, a family member, or a recent or upcoming event. You'll likely feel an emotion around the thing that comes to you. Notice physical sensations you have at the same time. You are observing the connection between a thought, a related emotion, and physical sensations. The goal here is to inform yourself of why you have the physical discomfort so you can address that issue. Just notice what comes up.

It's good to have paper or a journal next to you to write what that is. The writing movement of your hand is also a kind of release, and it gives another dimension of understanding around what you are feeling.

As you practice this, you are empowering yourself with more awareness of what is bothering you. It's so much more productive to address the cause rather than popping a pain reliever and lying down.

And more.

As you regularly move your body, and breathe calmly and deeply, you will often notice that your symptoms subside. Walk, go to the gym, run, climb, bike, hike—you know—the list is endless. But sitting in a chair will likely keep the discomfort, both physical and emotional, stuck right where it is.

With the movement and breathing, use your personal support mantra to shift your thoughts. Use the "think three things" exercise (from Mind 1) for the same reason. Open up to releasing the things you cannot control, focusing only on the things that you can.

For example, if you're scheduled to call on a client who is particularly unpleasant, focus on what you can accomplish during the meeting. Can you get some paperwork completed or create some other small positive results? What can you control that creates a positive outcome for you? Examples might be your breathing, choosing to smile, and monitoring your thoughts, and you could also set yourself up for a reward afterward. Maybe call on your favorite client next! Or stop for a cup of great coffee. Go for a quick walk in a lovely park. These are the things you can control.

Keep going. When this is new, it requires lots of practice! Happiness skills serve you better the more often you use them.

Sweet-Talk Your Body

We've talked about the power of words and thoughts. What you think is what you create! So when your body needs a little gratitude, put that into grateful thoughts and words and share it with your body. For example, try this: "Thank you, legs, for getting me around through this day. I know it's been a long one!" Or say, "Thank you, feet! I know you've been holding me up all day, and I appreciate you! We'll be home soon, and I'll soak you in an Epsom salts bath." Add a foot or leg self-massage too for extra appreciation.

If you have an injury or an illness, your positive thoughts work to support your natural healing processes.

I once had a client with a broken leg. She talked to her leg and healing bone often throughout the day.

"You're doing great, sweet bone! You're healing so quickly!" She would smile as she said it, amping up her healing energy and getting out of that cast in record time!

There are many stories and studies of people with illness, disease and injury using positive thought and imagery. Their positive body self-talk, visualizing healing and wellness, talking to their illness, their injury and their healthy cells, improves their recovery rates and their ability to manage therapies.

So be grateful to your body and encourage it. From a sore muscle to bigger things, encourage your body and express gratitude. Happiness skills support health and feeling good.

Take Regular Breaks

Pay attention to the signals your body sends you. For example, fidgeting is a signal that you need to get up and move. That's energy that needs to be released, or a block will build up to whatever you're doing. You'll become less effective as you "push through" it.

The same goes for discomfort. If you notice wanting to shift in your seat, maybe your shoulders are getting stiff and you need to stretch your neck; or maybe you're just uncomfortable, and it's time to get up and move. Take a few steps, wiggle and walk, stretch and bend, jump up and down. Your body will be refreshed and ready to continue with renewed engagement.

This also works when you find yourself becoming more easily distracted. Get up, move, walk, change the scene, "take five"!

Summary

The things I commit to doing

Check the yellow box for each Skill and Practice you are saying 'yes' to. ✔

- [ ] *What Is Your Body Telling You*

- [ ] *Sweet-Talk Your Body*

- [ ] *Take Regular Breaks*

Do you want to create reminders for any of these?

*There are several quick and easy skills
to practice that support happiness
through your body.*

We will look at some here, including touch. Your skin is a powerful recep-tor. As your skin notices sensations, it sends signals to your brain with information about what's happening: whether things feel good or not. Cold and hot, soft and rough, stimulating and calming, friend or foe, your skin is talking to you.

HAPPINESS SKILLS AND PRACTICES

Touch: For You and for Others

With that thought in mind, think about touch. Good touch. Nourishing touch like a caress, soft pats, comforting massage, which all release oxytocin from the brain, increasing feelings of well-being. Whether you are touching another person with a reassuring hand on the shoulder or giving yourself or a loved one a hand or leg massage, touch sends signals to the brain of support and well-being. Increase your happiness by giv-ing touch kindly to others and to yourself.

As you express gratitude to your body for carrying you around through life, give your legs, arms, hands, feet, and shoulders a massage. You'll in-crease relaxation and send signals of well-being to your brain. You can also schedule a massage for yourself.

Hugs!

Hugging yourself—yes, I said yourself—and others is a super touch nourisher! Put your arms around yourself and squeeze. Drop your head into your shoulder and hold that pose. Rest into this hug and feel the goodness in caring for yourself. Hugging in our culture seems to be more accepted than it once was and for good reason: it helps us all to thrive!

Touching with care and kindness is a happiness skill. Giving kind touch supports your happiness just as well as receiving touch. Practice comforting touch and notice the ease it can bring.

Breathe!

If you are a student of self-growth and energy work, then you are probably aware of the power of breathing with intention, which is breathing on purpose. What does that mean? Don't we just breath automatically? Yes, you're always breathing! Breathing on purpose is mindfully noticing your in-breath and your out-breath. As you focus, you are automatically restored to your center and to the present moment. Noticing your breath puts your focus on the here and now, which is the only place you actually have impact. You are only in one moment at a time, and it's this one! Clearly time past is out of reach, and the future, even the next second, is not yet here. The only moment you have any control over is the one you are in.

Many people have a habit of holding their breath. You may take a breath in while focusing intently on something and forget to let it out. This can also happen when you experience something upsetting and you literally hold your breath, forgetting to breathe out. Slow, even, deep breathing is how we are designed to take in air when we are not exerting ourselves physically. This kind of breathing also supports calm, peace, and ease.

Try this. Next time something comes along where you get upset, notice what happens to your breathing. Shallow breathing and holding your breath lead to your brain getting agitated. It wants more oxygen, and it's not getting it. This creates distress and dis-ease in your body.

When you notice this happening, shift to slow, deep, even breathing. Fully breathe in and out. As you exhale, let it out with the natural sounds of the exhale, loud and clear.

Let's imagine you're in a conversation with a friend. She's telling you about a fight that happened with her boyfriend, which is an oft-repeated story. Your first impulse is to get frustrated and upset because you've told her time and again that this relationship is a dead end. You check your breathing right in that moment, noticing your reaction. Then, instead of reacting, you simply slow your breath as you listen, breathing deeply and evenly. This gives your brain the oxygen it needs to remain calm. You are now able to stay separate from the story she is telling and simply listen. This takes practice, so keep at it.

You can listen then with detachment and get clear on how you want to respond. That's way better than getting upset!

Let go of wanting to jump into her story with comment or opinions. Instead, breathe.

Tip: Always default to three deep, slow, rib-expanding breaths when anything challenging comes along.

Look up!

It's that easy; look up. Whenever you need a lift, lift your face to the "sky." Lift your eyes up too. This works wherever you are—inside or out—lying down, standing, sitting, whatever.

This is a powerful shifter when you want to feel lighter, happier, more at ease. If you are noticing sadness and anxiety, look up. If you can increase the light around you by opening window shades, turning on lights, or going outside, do that too.

The motion of tilting our heads up, rolling our eyes skyward, and opening our eyes wider sends a signal to the brain that all is well. Consequently, we produce neurotransmitters that send a different set of signals to say, "I'm OK."

Now add this: Open your arms out wide to your sides and lift them up. Scoop in all the goodness of that upward glance!

Smile

Pretty simple really, smile! Smiling is a game changer. It's an instant happiness message to your brain and everyone who sees you smiling. So smile. Try it now. Sitting all alone and reading, smile. Notice how it changes your attitude and your energy. This is the good stuff. :)

Drink Water

OK, this is real. Your brain is not going to work as well if it's not hydrated! Grumpiness or flattening out sets in as your brain becomes dehydrated, which is happening way before you get thirsty. This affects all parts of your body, which is major since living in your best possible health is a true happiness choice. When it comes to your brain, being hydrated is the difference between feeling great and just feeling OK. So this is easy: Get a water bottle and keep filling it up; sixty-four ounces a day is optimal. Any amount more than you've been drinking is a great beginning! Work your way up!

> *TIP - How about having a glass of water one time each day instead of a coffee, tea, or soft drink? Remember that happiness skills are a practice, and you will come to love the new choices as you do them consistently. Stick with it!*

Arms up!

Lift your arms straight up over your head, clasp your hands together if that feels good, and arch your back. Look up and extend your body. Go for a few more inches in height as you stretch and extend. Breathe! This is a nice thing to do for your back. It also provides your head, heart, and whole body with a break. Nice!

Summary

The things I commit to doing

Check the yellow box for each Skill and Practice you are saying 'yes' to. ✔

☐ *Touch: For You and for Others*

☐ *Hugs!*

☐ *Breathe!*

☐ *Look up!*

☐ *Smile*

☐ *Drink Water*

☐ *Arms up!*

Do you want to create reminders for any of these?

Body 5

Your Relationship with Food

As you explore all aspects of yourself living in happiness, it's important to look at your relationship with food.

Is it a friendship and a joy or a struggle and a place of hiding? Do you ignore what you're eating or engage with food from love and appreciation?

Eating to feel energized, healthy, and vibrant is a self-care happiness practice. We each have a complex relationship with food. This is a big topic for many people, so let's talk about it with care and respect. As we grow our life in ways that truly resonate for us, that lift us and support us from our deepest values, our relationship with food becomes simpler. It becomes easier to think about our food choices in terms of the following:

energy

feeling good while we eat and after we eat

choosing simple foods that are whole and from the earth

growing a loving relationship of appreciation and gratitude with food

changing our palate

And that all adds up to awesome food love!

This is how I recommend you think about food:

> *As I practice amazing self-care and nourishment in mind, body, heart, and spirit, my food choices will naturally shift too. I am at ease in my body.*

Practice repeating that thought. This statement is reassuring and works to manifest your relationship with food from a place of happiness, joy, and nourishment for loving yourself. If this is a new way of thinking, remember it takes time, patience, and repetition to create change. Keep your thoughts to this simple phrase as you support yourself in practicing this happiness skill.

You'll notice I am not presenting a specific food education resource here. There are many wonderful resources available online, and there are videos to watch and books to read and listen to. Search "nutrition" online and see what resources speak to you. Go there and learn about how you can begin and continue to be conscious about choosing the foods you eat.

Some people have a healthy connection to food while others do not. As your happiness skills practice grows, there will be a natural shift in your relationship with food. I want to reassure you of this. Focusing on all aspects of you and of your life and practicing new ways of doing things will naturally shift all of you. The ripple effect!

Please take note here: Each person's relationship with food is very personal. Uninvited comments on what people eat and how they prepare and shop for food are best left unsaid. There are many emotions attached to food and eating. We are each on a separate journey, and tending to your own path is the job at hand. We will address letting go of trying to control others in Heart 5, You Can Only Control You. For now, make note of this concept and practice not commenting on the food choices of others.

HAPPINESS SKILLS AND PRACTICES

The Repeating Phrase

Post the recommended food thought phrase in places where you will see it often. This could be on your phone, desktop screensaver, lock screen image on your phone, bathroom mirror, office wall, or dashboard in your car. Where is a good place for you to see your reminders?

Write Your Food Mantra

Write a mantra about the way you envision your relationship with food. This will be helpful to recite as you approach snack and mealtime, to use as you shop at the market, or to focus on when you look at a menu in a restaurant.

Sample Food Mantras

"My mouth is happy (I feel happy) when I provide healthy foods that taste fresh and exciting. I choose an array of things that are satisfying to me and eat them until I am nourished and my stomach is comfortable. Yay, good food!"

"I trust and appreciate the food I eat. I am at peace and in gratitude as I slowly enjoy chewing each bite."

"I choose foods that I have fun with and enjoy—foods that I know will nourish my body!"

Now it's your turn. What is a good food mantra for you? What phrase comes to mind that reflects how you want your relationship with food to be? You can talk about what you choose to eat, where you choose to eat, and how and where you buy food. You want to include your vision of being comfortable and happy with food and what that feels like before, during, and after eating. It's a vision statement for you to see yourself happy in friendship with food.

The point of the food mantra is to retrain your brain to encourage eating for health and happiness instead of escape or distraction. As we talked about in the Mind section, words are powerful. The words we choose to think will be our truth. As we repeat them, they become a belief. So use the good ones to support yourself with food.

Now it's your turn. What's a good food mantra for you?

Use this space to write your food mantra.

_____

_____

_____

_____

_____

_____

_____

_____

As with your personal support mantra and the repeating phrase, post your food mantra for easy access and memorization.

On a personal note, the word "no" is not in my vocabulary around food. If there's something I want, I take my time and make the choice to eat it with the intention of loving myself and enjoying the experience. I pause, choose what I want, then enjoy it completely. As I have grown in this work, I have also grown into being peaceful with food. It has been an unexpected, lovely side effect of healing my heart with happiness skills practices!

Summary

Check the yellow box for each Skill and Practice you are saying 'yes' to. ✔

The things I commit to doing

☐ The Repeating Phrase

☐ Write Your Food Mantra

☐ Use It Often!

Do you want to create reminders for any of these?

Body Happiness Skills Summary

Would you like to highlight the ones you are saying yes to?

THE POWER OF MOVEMENT

Moving in Figure Eights

Tai Chi, Tai Ji, Qigong, Yoga

The Reset

Hands to Heart

Hands to Stomach

Centering

Stand Straight, Shoulders Back, Chin up

Move!

GROUNDING: THE POWER OF STILLNESS

Mountain Pose

Lie on the Ground

Get in Your Heels

Breathe Slowly and Deeply

BODY VOICES

What Is Your Body Telling You?

Sweet-Talk Your Body

Take Regular Breaks

SUPPORTING YOURSELF

Touch: For You and for Others

Hugs!

Breathe!

Look up!

Smile

Drink Water

Arms up!

YOUR RELATIONSHIP WITH FOOD

The Repeating Phrase

Write Your Food Mantra

Use it often!

Self-Love

It took me the longest time to figure out what self-love is, what it feels like, if it's OK, or what!

I understood that it was important, well kind of, anyway, but for the life of me I couldn't figure out how to feel it. I was pretty well conditioned not to notice myself, for many reasons (and that's another book), so loving myself in theory sounded OK, but there was some work to do to get there!

How about you? Where are you with this concept? Do you feel numb or blank when you check in on loving yourself? Do you feel connected to the idea? Or do you think, "Wow that's messed up. I don't get this idea of loving me!"

It's only in more recent years that I've gotten to this place of being in a loving relationship with myself. As I have more actively created the life that aligns with my purpose and values, I have learned to have fun with me! I've become my own best company as I pursue a fulfilling list of what's important in each day, and part of that list is self-care. Loving yourself includes self-care, not self-absorption. It's not ego focused; it's care focused. Self-care is about supporting yourself in countless ways and enjoying who you are, which is part of this great continuum of building love for you and enjoying being you.

Cultivating self-love is first and foundational in developing your happiness skills. If you think of happiness as something you create from a recipe, a main ingredient is love for yourself. From there it's possible to practice and solidly ground all of your happiness skills. Cultivation of a loving relationship with yourself may feel foreign or "self-centered." This is not the case. Instead, it is a means of living as your best self, expanding all that's good in you, and your happiness. This in turn is better for everyone around you. As with all of the happiness skills, the practices of self-love require commitment. Some of the things you've already read will move you toward this loving commitment, and there are a few more skills and practices to learn here.

HAPPINESS SKILLS AND PRACTICES

What Do You Value about You?

Hmmm, good question, huh? Maybe it's your ability to talk with people or your kindness toward others. Perhaps you're a good athlete or you like how you look in your new jeans! You might be a really good speller or good at remembering birthdays. What else? Think creatively here! What are the things you value about you?

Make a list of the things you value and appreciate about yourself.

Take your time and really think. This is only for you to read, so put it all here!

_____

_____

_____

_____

_____

_____

_____

_____

_____

_____

_____

_____

Next, using Post-it Notes or index cards, copy the items from your list—one per card.

Make them cool or pretty or awesome so you like the way they look. If you're neat and precise, make them neat and precise. If you like color and design, get creative and bring that to the cards. Maybe you want to make them in your computer, print them out, and cut them into fun shapes.

The goal is to have affirmations and reminders for you of what you value about yourself. When you start to get in a slump and feel like you're lost or just burned out, these cards can help bring you back to yourself in a loving and supportive way, as your own best friend.

Post a few of these where you can see them each day. Rotate your cards frequently to keep your perspective fresh. You can also set reminders in your phone that say your affirmations to you. These visual reminders will encourage the thought patterns to develop in your brain around self-acceptance, love, and appreciation for you! Add to this list as your happiness grows.

Being Your Own Best Friend

When I was eighteen years old I got a book called *How to Be Your Own Best Friend*. I knew it was important, but little did I know that the messages in that wonderful book foreshadowed a life path for me. Messages like this: "We must realize that we have a choice, we are responsible for our own happiness." And this: "People think happiness is something that happens to them, they don't realize there are things they have to do." I heard the message loud and clear: My happiness was my own responsibility and an action was required, though I was still clueless how to get there! It took many years of practicing to learn to love and support myself, developing tools that I'm sharing here, to fully walk the path of happiness.

I want you to understand that being your own best friend sets you up to grow your self-love and caring practices. Being the one who listens to you, loves you without condition, and is always there to help—that's a best friend. Be that for yourself and think about this: If someone was to ask who your best friend is, how would it feel to say "me"?

Practice that in front of a mirror.

"Who's your best friend? Me!"

Do it again, again, and again! Good! Let this be a new mantra for you:

"I am my own best friend!"

Self-Nurture, Self-Care

Please revisit the skills and practices in the Body section's chapter 4, Supporting Yourself. Happiness skills are interdependent since they work with all aspects of your whole being.

Here are some reminders:

massaging your feet

take a warm bath

doing things you love to do

laughing

resting

movement

good nourishment

hugging yourself

slow, easy breathing

Cultivating Self-Love

Practice 1: Connecting with Your Younger Self

Connecting with self-love can be simple. Think of the deep nurturing and love you have felt for a pet, a child, or a baby you have held. Anything you have ever felt that deep, caring love for. Now take that sense of caring and imagine holding yourself as a baby. If you have some pictures of yourself as a baby or a small child, put those where you can see them often. Images like that can be very helpful for this visualization. Get in touch with little you and imagine holding yourself. It may be easier to close your eyes as you're imagining this. See the place where you're sitting and what you have on as a baby or small child, and feel the temperature in the room and see what's around you. Hear the sounds you make as a child.

Feel that sense of deep caring for this little version of you. Feel what your inner child needs. Perhaps loving words, to be held, or to ask a question. As you visualize this version of yourself, ask your younger self, "What do you need to feel happy and safe?" The answers will come with practice. Sit quietly and be present. Begin a conversation with little you, offering reassurance and support. This is a first step and a good practice to continue. Trust yourself to show up and love your younger self. If this feels awkward to you, tap into the love and kindness you'd give to any child and try again.

*Here's an example of how the
conversation might go.*

*You sit quietly, perhaps closing your eyes, and take three
deep breaths in and out.*

Relax your body and become present.

*Visualize yourself as a child sitting with you and ask, "What do you need
to feel happy and safe." Or you may choose to ask another question.*

You may "hear" from the child, "I'm scared; I'm not good enough."

*Your response could be this: "I understand. You are perfect as you are.
You are more than enough."*

Begin this practice and keep going until your child grows in trust, in a feeling of safety, or whatever feeling he or she needs. Keep the visits and conversation going, and as you do that, journal what you learn about yourself. As you support your inner child, your adult self will evolve those feelings, too, growing your self-acceptance, trust, ease, and, yes, self-love.

There can be feelings that come up for you here that help you to commit your love and nurturing to your adult self. It's a powerful practice indeed. Use your journal to process what you notice as you do this practice.

Practice 2: Fun Alone Time with You!

Choose to spend time alone doing things you enjoy! This practice is to cultivate having fun with yourself. Notice what it's like having fun with yourself and enjoying being with you! Through this awareness you reinforce what you like about yourself and how time for fun with your own interests is important. Make time for this regularly, and schedule it in your planner. Again, journal about the experiences you have. Include all details that feel important to you, including how you feel.

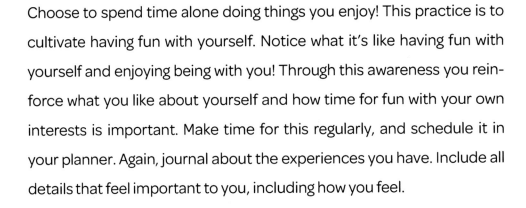

Practice 3: How Are You Doing Loving Yourself?

As you make yourself a top priority in your life, journal how it feels to have fun with you and connect with yourself in this caring way. To check on the quality of your connection to loving self, imagine for a moment that you were left alone in your life for whatever reason. Would you be able to feel a sense of safety in being with yourself and in caring for and being good company for yourself?

You are your most important living human being. This is your most important role (remember roles from Mind 4?). You need yourself for love, care, and support every day! So look for the ways you're doing this. Maybe it's noticing you're tired during the day, so you make time for a ten-minute power nap in your car. Perhaps it's being sure that you get your ten minutes in the morning for meditation and ten more for journaling. Feel the way this self-care lands in your body, in your core. Does it feel good to you?

As you grow this quality of connection, check in with yourself by closing your eyes, quieting your mind, quieting your body, and asking, "How does it feel in me and around me as I receive my own self-care?"

Journal what you notice and how you are progressing with this practice and awareness. This may feel awkward at first, but keep going. Growing your enjoyment and appreciation of yourself is key to your best life.

Summary

The things I commit to doing

Check the yellow box for each Skill and Practice you are saying 'yes' to. ✔

☐ What Do You Value about You?

☐ Being Your Own Best Friend

☐ Self-Nurture, Self-Care

☐ Cultivating Self-Love

☐ Connecting with Your Younger Self

☐ Fun Alone Time with You!

☐ How Are You Doing Loving Yourself

Do you want to create reminders for any of these?

The Power of Connection

People are naturally designed to connect with other people. To be happy, we need a sense of being part of something more than ourselves, so we create relationships with people and things that allow us to go beyond ourselves.

For connection to bring happiness, it must feel purposeful and rewarding and involve kindness and acceptance. Creating connections that feel fulfilling, purposeful, and joyful is a happiness skill.

Some of us are very connected in our lives in a variety of ways, and for others connection is more limited. You may currently be connected in ways that drain you, that deplete your sense of well-being and happiness. This is not the desirable means of connecting I'm referring to. As you develop your happiness skills, you will be making changes that keep you focused on positive, satisfying connections.

Let's look at how connection, relationships, and love all work together.

Relationships

Connection creates relationships. If you buy pots of flowers to put around your house, you've begun a relationship through caring for those flowers, and they in turn bring you pleasure. They win; you win. This is a relationship built on care and from a source of enjoyment chosen intentionally by you.

Relationships exist when any two or more things or people are connected by a link such as caring and enjoyment. Much like pots of flowers, you may have a pet to which you're connected by the mutual benefit you receive from each other. You chose to have this pet, and the emotional connection began. You hope for love, affection, and fun from your pet, and you give love, care, and affection in return. It's a mutually satisfying exchange. The connections that support your happiness bring many things: kindness, appreciation, love, fun, support, understanding, joy—the list is long!

In the movie *Eat Pray Love*, Liz Gilbert says she is having a relationship with her pizza. She is connecting to her pizza. The connector there is the emotion of joy, delight, and passionate appreciation she is receiving through her sense of taste. That's connection too.

The world is full of possibilities for connection. Look at nature: animals, plants, and other living things. Nature and the outdoors are so full of living things to connect to that it's impossible to count them all. The air is a living thing, along with the sun, the moon, the stars. These are all resources that are full of active energy, ever changing and activating aliveness in so much. Trees, rocks, bugs large and small, microscopic life. It's all available for you to be in relationship with. You've only to open your awareness to connect through appreciation and joy—a warmth in your body that connects you with all things.

Connection with people can happen in many ways. Consider digital communication; there's Facebook, FaceTime, email, texting, and too many apps to mention! Phones, computers, and other digital electronics allow us to see and hear one another from great distances and through other barriers that once demanded detachment. We can connect with and meet people we never would have otherwise and receive nourishment of shared stories and interests that are, that's right, connection!

HAPPINESS SKILLS AND PRACTICES

Connect!

With your focus on making connection with things that you enjoy, let's begin with a simple awareness exercise. I invite you to make a list of everything you can think of that you feel connected to in a positive way. Write everything you can think of—large, small, common, unusual. This is your personal list.

Examples are as follows:

People who nourish your life, that you enjoy being with. Family, friends, coworkers, and even acquaintances! Yes, and pets. :)

Things in nature: trees, clouds, sun, flowers, animals; you get the idea, stuff outside!

Your home and other places you enjoy being such as your car, church, yoga studio, and meditation spot!

Activities such as bike riding, rock climbing, sewing, creating something, singing, you know, stuff you like to do!

Other things, such as inanimate objects that are important to you. Clothing that's special to you, things you own or see as you go through your days. Stuff!

Make your list here:

_____

_____

_____

_____

_____

_____

_____

_____

_____

_____

_____

Now that you have this list and you've brought your attention to the people and things that bring you smiles, happiness, and joy, choose three things or people to interact with each day—to see, communicate with, or interact with, be with. This assures a happy buzz from making the connection. Cool, right? Happiness is using your skills, and this is a great one to focus on.

Relationships with People

The practice here is to create, choose, and invest time in relationships that are fulfilling and satisfying. Relationships that nourish you and support you.

What does this mean? These relationships are with people who listen with acceptance, who do not offer advice unless they're asked, who love you without condition. This also includes people who like you without condition. People who live from a positive life perspective, who take responsibility for themselves and their happiness. People like you, right? This is the goal. To grow into this person and surround yourself with people who are the same way.

You may be in relationships with people who do not fit this description. When people start the Happiness Is a Skill work and take a closer look at their relationships, they often notice the negative people in their lives—those who deplete their energy. These are people who create difficult feelings rather than easy, satisfying feelings and experiences. Worse, they may be longtime friends and even family members.

In section Mind 3 you read about Limbic Resonance. This comes up again here. Your happiness is directly affected by the resonance, or the lack of resonance which is dissonance, of others around you: the mood they are in. This is reflected in the words they say, their body posture and movements, which convey the energy that is present in them. Your otherwise happy state will begin to wobble and shift] when you are around people who are negative in thought, mood, words and actions.

A favorite quote that addresses this is from Jill Bolte Taylor: "Be responsible for the energy you bring into the room."

HAPPINESS SKILLS AND PRACTICES

Relationship Boundaries

 First, observe your relationships. Journal or otherwise make note of the positive, uplifting, kind, and supportive people you spend time with, and do the same with the negative people.

Second, consider ways to increase time with the positive people and decrease time with the negative ones. I know that sounds simplistic. But keeping it simple is important. As you limit time with people on the negative side of this list, you may decide to remove them from your list altogether.

You may say, "But my mom is one of the most critical, negative people in my life, and I have to spend time with her. She's sick and alone. I'm all she has."

Or you may say that your boss is always complaining and yelling and that you can't stay away from your boss.

That brings us to boundaries. This is a key word for your happiness skills practice.

Let's go right to examples.

In the case of the mom situation, a boundary can look like many things. The first thing to introduce is honesty with carefully chosen words.

In an effort to set a boundary with Mom, a conversation could go like this:

"Mom, I've been learning about how to bring more happiness into my life. I've learned that using positive words and having positive people to be around is a big part of being happy. For example, I'm practicing positive words right now as I talk with you. Could we do this together?"

Mom says, "I don't know what you're talking about. I feel awful all of the time, and I'm stuck here at home. What do I have to be positive about?"

Your response could be this: "I'm here now. I come to visit which gives you something to look forward to and enjoy, so that's a good thing, Mom. The more positive we make this, the more we will want to share time together.

"How about we try something new, Mom? Let's play a game of (fill in whatever game you want here. Could be a word game, cards, a board game)."

Key Points:

1. You continue to come back with a positive counterpoint and a subject change like suggesting the game.

2. Try that two to three times. If the other person continues to resist this concept you're introducing, go to the next step.

3. "I understand this may take time for you to embrace, Mom. Making changes to be happier is important to me, so I have to follow through with that. I'm going to go now, as that's part of what I'm learning too. Maybe you can think more about how we can be positive and enjoy our time together. I love you, and I hope to spend more good time and happy time together. Let's try this again next time."

4. You continue to repeat only what you are going to create now in your life rather than being drawn into rehashing and negativity.

5. You do not allow the old negative patterns of entangled conversation to pull you in. Do not respond to any of those lead-ins. Simply go to point 3 above and say your goodbyes for now.

In the example of your boss, here are some things to practice.

Key Points:

1. Imagine you're sitting through a tough meeting with your boss, whether one-on-one or in a group. He's going on about what's wrong in the company; he always has a list. This is when you tune your ears to targeted listening for key points. You're looking for the key points through the negative wording. A metaphor could be digging through a bucket of dirt, knowing that there are a couple of valuable things in there that you need. You ignore the dirt and focus on finding what you need.

Remember this: What you think, is what you create. Focus on what matters in terms of you doing your job to your satisfaction. Listen for what you need to know and leave the rest.

2. Another practice you could use here is reframing. Do this by hearing what is being said and reframing how it could be said in a positive way. This can be fun and a good practice to distract from the negativity.

   For example, your boss says, "Since our sales are down again this quarter, I'm sure we're going to stay stuck in this trend."

   And you reframe that in your mind to say, "Let's brain storm three things we can do to reverse this sales trend."

3. Your third practice is to limit the time you have to be with the boss. Use email when you can do that instead of meeting, and shorten up in-person contacts when you can. Minutes matter. If possible, anticipate what this person will need before he or she asks. This could minimize communication.

4. Use your personal support mantra and breathe before, during, and after the time with someone who challenges you. If you must spend extended time around that person, take as many short breaks in your thoughts as you can, use your breathing, and release tension in your body. Perhaps think about a visit to a favorite spot, seeing yourself doing something you love to do. You get the idea; a quick, distracting thought journey to your fishing cabin can keep you grounded.

5. When you are done with such an interaction, remember this: eyes up, smile, do the reset. Choose which happiness skills you want to use to walk away with and leave that negativity behind you!

Love

When it comes to connection, this is the "mother lode." I mean loving without expectation, loving as a form of energy that nurtures, accepts, and supports without condition. This creates the highest level of connection.

Notice the use of "without expectation" and "accepts without condition."

These terms describe where the power of loving kindness creates the strongest bond of connection. Consider this: When you say "I love you," do you mean that you are offering this without expectation or condition—as a gift? The answer to this question may not be obvious. Using the skills of self-observation and journaling, what do you notice about your way of offering love? Answering this will help you to bring more loving kindness to the people and things you love—to be an even more loving person and better fulfill a key value.

HAPPINESS SKILLS AND PRACTICES

Observe Yourself

Observe yourself. What do you notice about how you give and receive love? Is it in words or in deeds? Are you sharing without condition, or do you expect something in return? Do you offer love with expectations of the person you love? What words do you use? Is it, for example, "I love you when you're smiling," or simply, "I love you, and I love your smile." The first one puts a condition on your love; the second comment affirms the other person with love and without condition.

Journal Your Observations

Journal what you like and don't like about how you express love, how you feel love, and how you offer love. Also journal any thoughts about how you'd like to be loving in new ways. What's here for you as you observe yourself?

Summary

The things I commit to doing

Check the yellow box for each Skill and Practice you are saying 'yes' to.

☐ *Connect!*

☐ *Relationship Boundaries*

☐ *Observe Yourself*

☐ *Journal Your Observations*

Do you want to create reminders for any of these?

GIVING

Contributing, giving, or doing something for someone is a happiness skill.

This can be something big or small, depending on your time and what and to whom you want to contribute. You may want to make a long-term commitment as a volunteer, such as a court-appointed special advocate, or CASA, for children needing someone to be present in their lives. You may simply want to lend a smile or a quick hello to someone who is lonely and looking down.

The important thing for you to know is that you have gifts, talents, and knowledge, and the world needs all of that! These offerings from you can come from stories you've collected, lessons you've learned, skills you have, optimism you possess, and energy you spread to others. It may be smiling, saying a kind word, giving a handshake, or providing a hug. The ability to listen and give someone your attention is among the greatest gifts you can offer. Your gifts are needed to assist someone else, to land in the right place at the perfect moment.

How about making hats for women on chemo who have lost their hair, or blankets for babies who have been abandoned? Maybe you love wood crafting, photography, or cooking. Your creations can make people's lives better. Consider writing something that matters to you and post it online or in a publication. It will matter to someone else too. Donating money can be helpful, and while financial contributions are certainly important, ask yourself, "Is there a more personal way I can share and give to others?" If you're good with numbers, then perhaps you might allocate some time to volunteering to help with budgets and bookwork or to simply driving the elderly and delivering meals to people who can't get out. Find a need and give of yourself in some way. It will fill you up!

Giving occurs when you're brave, when you say "yes" to trying something new, to putting yourself out in some way. Sometimes giving occurs when you choose a little discomfort or inconvenience for the good of another person. When this is done as a way of living in alignment with your own values, then you both win!

My brother-in-law teaches painting classes. This is a talent he came across later in his life. He practiced his skills with dedication until he was ready to offer this to others. His students find a new confidence in themselves, and they learn the joy of creating something tangible through the uplifting experience of personal growth! Now, that's giving.

How about the woman who takes her dog to the retirement home to give the residents the joy of spending time with a warm and caring friend? Or the man in my neighborhood who makes it his business to quietly pick up any wayward trash each morning on his walk? How do you want to contribute?

Let me assure you that when you stop an impulse to share or do for someone or something because you think you don't bring value, or no one will care what you have to share, or you're afraid to be embarrassed or rejected, then that's when you do it anyway! You say, "Yes I can, and yes I will!" Be brave. You'll be glad you were.

HAPPINESS SKILLS AND PRACTICES

Make a Commitment to Give

OK, here we go! Action time! What are you going to commit to giving, beginning now? These need to be things that feel resonant, fulfilling, possible. Have you been thinking of volunteering in some form and have been putting it off? Be creative and expand your thinking. Be a little adventurous, too, opting possibly for something that pushes you a little out of your comfort zone. It can even be something simple.

Make a list of what you would like to commit to doing and the action steps you would need to take to learn more about this.

1. I want to commit to

_____

Action steps I need to take:

_____

_____

_____

2. I want to commit to

_____

Action steps I need to take:

_____

_____

_____

_____

3. I want to commit to

_____

Action steps I need to take:

_____

_____

_____

_____

4. I want to commit to

_____

Action steps I need to take:

_____

_____

_____

_____

5. I want to commit to

_____

Action steps I need to take:

_____

_____

_____

_____

6. I want to commit to

_____

Action steps I need to take:

_____

_____

_____

_____

7. I want to commit to

_____

Action steps I need to take:

_____

_____

_____

_____

Now that you have your list, put these action steps in your planner and start giving in the ways you enjoy.

Set Your Intention

During your morning practices, set your intention to give in some way during the day. You can make a statement that could be to give a ride to a family member, send a nice text greeting to an old friend, or go by your coworker's office with a cup of coffee. Perhaps the intention you need to set today is to give in some way to yourself.

Visualize yourself giving in ways that matter to you. This may be something small. It may also be taking a step to follow through on the commitments you put on your commitment list. Write in your journal about your intentions to give.

RECEIVING

Receiving with appreciation is a happiness skill and a way of giving. When the person on the other end of your giving receives what you have given, that too is a kind of gift! It completes the circle of caring and appreciation that generates happiness for all parties.

Imagine you are volunteering to cook at the homeless shelter. The people coming through the line for the meal you've prepared are grateful; they clearly need this food. They are receiving because of your time and effort, and that feels good to you.

When you give a gift to someone and that person lights up with smiles, you are practicing the happiness skill of giving. By the same token, when you receive a gift with grace and appreciation, that is a happiness skill too.

Happiness Skills and Practices

Receiving is often overlooked. The practice is to notice yourself as opportunities to receive come up. Are you comfortable receiving? Do you tend to hesitate, pull back, or try to avoid the receiving because you're uncomfortable? Whether it's a simple cup of coffee from a coworker or opening gifts at a surprise birthday party, what do you notice about your reaction to receiving?

Check in, too, with how you feel receiving compliments and affection? How is your comfort level there? This is an important question to write about in your journal.

Notice Your Feelings

Notice your feelings around receiving. You may not be comfortable receiving. What's there for you, inside of you? What is there behind the discomfort? This difficulty is often about your self-worth. To receive is to acknowledge that you are worthy of receiving. That you are valuable. That you are enough. Using your journal, process what's there for you. Refer back to section Heart 1 on self-love. After all, receiving is a way of you loving you too.

If you notice discomfort or resistance with receiving, notice how you are actually giving too. The person giving to you is literally receiving as much or more than you are. Remember that these are mutually beneficial exchanges.

Set Your Intention

Set your intention to receive. During your morning practices, you may write or say, "My intention today is to be present with receiving. I want to be aware of the power of this important practice for myself and people who wish to give to me. My intention is to receive gracefully."

Notice how this goes throughout your day. What showed up? How did you practice your intention? These are good questions to journal about.

Ask for What You Need

Maybe you need comfort, support, intimacy, or companionship as you do something like go for a walk. A friend to be with is a happiness tool. Asking that friend for what you need leads to receiving, and it gives the friend the opportunity to give to you. Reach out to people in your life such as a family member, coworker, coach, or anyone who is available to you, and ask for what you need. You'll never know what's possible until you ask.

Saying Yes and Saying No

Taking care of your well-being is always first and foremost throughout happiness skills practice. This is a guiding thought when you're offered a gift or assistance of any kind.

In making choices about giving and receiving, you say yes to the good stuff and no to the things that don't serve you. We've already learned many practices that care for and support you. We've learned that changing your default setting to saying "yes!" to what you like and what you want to have in your life is part of this mindset.

Apply this idea to receiving. You are going to say "no!" to the things and experiences that do not support you and lift you up—to things that are not good for you. If someone is offering or giving you something that does not feel right, then you will politely decline whatever it is that the person is offering.

This is a big point, so I want to spend a minute here. You have the right and the responsibility in caring for yourself to say no to the things that do not support you and lift you up in your life. If someone wants you to accept or do something and is asking or coaxing you into something he or she wants you to accept or to do that does not resonate for you, then you practice saying "no." This can be a big change, so you may need to start small and work your way up to being consistent. As with all practices, baby steps and a renewed commitment each day are the key.

In your journal, record specific instances of saying yes to the things that are good for you and no to the things that are not. Write down the outcome too. Maybe you've committed to yourself to get more sleep, so you say "no" to that last hour of TV at night and go to bed earlier. Perhaps someone asked you to go out to a party, and you don't really enjoy the people, and parties aren't fun to you. Normally you would say "yes" because you don't want to offend anyone. Now you realize that spending that same time getting caught up on things at home—or going out to do what you really love instead—is the right answer for you.

As you journal about these experiences and notice the outcome, it may take you time to grow your comfort with saying no. You may have a long history of people-pleasing. While that may have brought you a sense of relief or "rightness" in the past, it's important to check in and make sure you are fully honoring your own values and needs in saying yes. That's the point of this: to provide for yourself what you need first, which keeps you in balance with respect to giving to and receiving from others.

Giving and receiving are equally important. Making sure you're cared for first is key to doing all things well, including giving. Think about the instruction from the flight attendant on airplanes: always put your own oxygen mask on first. This is so you are well enough to provide the oxygen mask for others who may need help. That's you giving to and receiving from yourself. Practice on!

Summary

The things I commit to doing

Check the yellow box for each Skill and Practice you are saying 'yes' to. ✔

 *Make a Commitment to Give*

 *Set Your Intention to Give*

 *Notice Your Feelings*

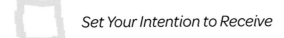 *Set Your Intention to Receive*

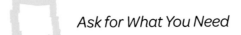 *Ask for What You Need*

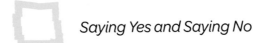 *Saying Yes and Saying No*

Do you want to create reminders for any of these?

Gratitude instantly softens your body, slows your heart rate, and deepens your breathing. It's a reset all by itself.

Your thoughts go to the good, and your heart warms in your chest. Such is the power of gratitude that it creates health through ease, joy, and appreciation. We've talked about the power of positive words, and this one practice delivers them in abundance.

With each grateful thought, we open new neural pathways. Yes, this is brain "rewiring" in action! Messages of well-being are transferred through your entire body, strengthening resilience with each thought. It's resilience that manifests emotionally, spiritually, and physically. New optimism is created, and you become more open to connection and compassion. All of that adds to your happiness, vitality, and well-being.

There are several skills and practices for gratitude, so let's get to it!

HAPPINESS SKILLS AND PRACTICES

Think Grateful Thoughts

When you notice your mind has free time, think grateful thoughts. This is especially good when you're going to sleep and as first thoughts when you wake up.

Grateful thoughts can be tiny things like your favorite towel, sneakers, or toothbrush. It can be that you have a dishwasher to wash your dishes, are expecting a baby, or have a cell phone and the many things you enjoy about that. You may be grateful for the color of the sky, money in your pocket, and a job that puts it there!

Also, there are the people you share life with that bring the really good stuff!

Opportunities for gratitude are endless indeed when you get into the details of your life—the things, people, and places to be grateful for. Remember to be grateful for your incredible body and how you are able to be here and do cool stuff like breathe. Be grateful for your whole self, warts and all! You're the only you there is, and that's cool.

Me? I'm endlessly grateful for my pillows and sheets and for getting enough sleep!

Embody Gratitude

Not feeling so good? Anxious, down, feeling blue? Here is a natural pairing of skills for immediate relief.

1. Stand up!

2. Look up by tilting your head back—chin up, eyes up.

3. Think about all you are grateful for:

   "I'm so grateful for this new day, the amazing sun shining on me, and the perfect cool breeze on my face. I'm so grateful for my spouse and children, for the warm water in my shower, and for the TV show I get to come home and watch tonight."

4. Add movement. Walk if you can. Keep going and stay with the grateful thoughts.

Write It Down: Your Gratitude Journal

1. As you go to bed each night, write down three to five things you are grateful for from that day, in that moment.

   Something like this: *"I'm super grateful for my old pair of tan hiking socks when I'm sitting on the sofa at night."*

   "I'm crazy grateful for my dog following me around the house and looking out for me."

   "I have a window that looks toward a beautiful tree outside. Every time I turn my head that way, I am grateful for what I see."

   It's important to have a journal or notebook on your nightstand as your gratitude journal. You can write the same things over and over each night or add whatever is significant for that day, that moment.

   You may want to get a special spiral or journal and decorate the cover in some way that indicates this is your gratitude journal. Making small things fun and special is a happiness skill too!

2. Now write three to five things you are grateful to yourself for each day. For example:

   "I'm grateful I got the groceries today." "I'm glad I completed a project at work." "I felt good stopping to help someone today." Anything—be it large, small, simple, or complex—can provide opportunities for gratitude. What will you put on your list?

A to Z

This is a great one. Write an alphabet list of things you are grateful for and read an item from this list at the beginning of each day. That gives you twenty-six days of gratitude to start with.

When you've gone through those, you can start again! You can write a new list at the end of those twenty-six days, with all new entries. Repeating is OK too.

You'll get into this kind of free-flowing gratitude in no time!

Grateful for Things Large and Small

Here are a few more ideas for your gratitude list:

- The lady bug that crossed your path that you didn't step on

- The plates in your cupboard

- The rain that makes your garden grow

- The car in your garage

- The nice neighbor across the street

- All sorts of people in your life

- Your spiritual beliefs and support

- Your nail file, especially when you have a broken nail!

- Also, your Mom or Dad, your children, your education, the place where you live

What things, large or small, are you grateful for?

As you journal about the things you are grateful for, let loose and go for it. When you stop to consider, you'll find all kinds of things. Even the hard stuff can have silver linings when you look for them, and hey, silver linings are awesome!

Say It Out Loud

Remember to share your gratitude with those in your life. Say it out loud to yourself, in your room, in your car—anywhere and everywhere you are. Say it out loud or by text or in a note to others. Share the energy of gratitude and watch it spread to the consciousness of people around you. Do this, and you'll wire your brain to be grateful every day!

You

The work of creating your happiness is about loving yourself. This is a deep happiness skills principle. It's about healing what hurts and living what feels true and fulfilling to you. So be grateful for yourself—for your body that gets you around, that keeps you here and alive. Be grateful for your heart, which guides you to read books like this and keeps you striving to find your best path. Be grateful for your spirit and your mind, which work together to make sense of your life and to live into happiness. When you are in those moments, the whole world wins. Happy, grateful people share their resonance with everyone around them.

That's a big win for everyone!

Again, chapter Heart 3 comes to mind here.

Feeling grateful! :)

Summary

The things I commit to doing

Check the yellow box for each Skill and Practice you are saying 'yes' to. ✔

- ☐ *Think Grateful Thoughts*

- ☐ *Embody Gratitude*

- ☐ *Write It Down: Your Gratitude Journal*

- ☐ *A to Z*

- ☐ *Grateful for Things Large and Small*

- ☐ *Say It Out Loud*

- ☐ *You*

Do you want to create reminders for any of these?

Being Your Best Self

*Being your best self
is heart work.*

When you're happy, your best self naturally shines through, and when you are living from your best self, you are happy. It's like the chicken and the egg; which comes first? Let's say they go together.

So what is our best self? Is this a judgment, a measuring stick, or a guideline?

No, it isn't any of these. Being your best self refers to you being in harmony with you. Living in synchronicity with you. Your best self is happy, fulfilled, at ease, balanced, and breathing deeply. It's you feeling alive and happy to be here, bringing all of your gifts to the world.

Each skill and practice that you choose from this handbook brings you closer to your own sustainable happiness. A happy heart opens you to your potential and helps you live as your best you, which is a gift to everyone around you, not to mention the world as a whole!

There are a few happiness skills I want to touch on around "best self."

They are as follows:

Feeling Accomplished

Deep Listening

Being Flexible

You Can Only Control You

FEELING ACCOMPLISHED

Let's start with feeling accomplished, which creates the sense of fulfillment that is key in living your best, happiest life. Maybe you're a person who thrives when checking off the items on a to-do list. Perhaps you relish the moment you complete a long-term goal. Maybe you helped your kids get their homework done last night. Regardless of what you accomplish, you feel good.

The skills and practices designed to support accomplishment are a kind of check-in that you can do with yourself throughout the day, the week, or the month. It's part of keeping an eye on living your purpose, your goals, and the action items that fulfill that purpose. Feeling accomplished can be tied to something as simple as noticing that you watered your plants or as complex as completing a big project you've been working on for many months. It's about being aware of what you are doing and creating ways to activate that awareness.

HAPPINESS SKILLS AND PRACTICE

Being Aware of Your Accomplishments

Activating awareness to notice what you've accomplished throughout the day can take several forms. For some people it might involve checking things off a to-do list or in a planner. For other people this might be a simple pause to notice and be aware of what they've done, like when they stop for a cup of coffee and think about their day. Consider making a list of what you have accomplished as you take a noontime break, and then again at the end of the day. Choose the techniques that feel best to you so that you'll stay committed to using them.

How do you want to create your feeling of accomplishment?

A. Use your planner and check things off there.

B. Create a to-do list that you write either the night before or in the morning, and check things off there.

C. Pause throughout your day and think through what you've accomplished as a simple practice of noticing and being aware. You can set a reminder in your phone to do this.

D. List what you have accomplished at preset intervals throughout the day. Set your phone timer or alarm to remind you to check in.

E. Work from a pile of tasks on your desk or in your work space. As you complete something, move it either to the trash or file it. You'll feel good seeing the pile get smaller

F. Design your own way of noticing accomplishments specific to the activities that fill your time. If it's folding laundry, then notice the pile of folded clothes. It it's serving tables in a restaurant, count your completed checks at the end of your shift. If you're a professional seeing clients in your office, review your appointment calendar at the end of the day and appreciate how much you completed.

DEEP LISTENING

Listening to others is perhaps the single greatest gift we can give. Deep listening is a clear expression that what someone is saying is important, that their thoughts and opinions have value. This in turn conveys the message that they are important.

Notice I said deep listening. What is that? Deep listening is when you are managing your own busy mind so that you are fully present with that person. Deep listening requires that you focus word-for-word on what is being said—not allowing yourself to get stuck on one thing the person says, then waiting to say something about that. If you do that, you won't hear the rest of what is being said. That isn't listening; that's taking the moment back from the person and wanting to create your own. That's you wanting your idea to be heard rather than listening.

Deep listening is being present as a witness to another person's sharing without being attached to what the person says. This is called "holding space." In this role you are not judging or forming opinions; nor are you offering any advice or feedback. You are simply quiet, listening deeply.

If you are asked for feedback, you keep your response specific to the question and to the point. Less is more when it comes to feedback. Practice condensing your responses into fewer, more concise words for clarity. Asking follow-up questions that show interest and a desire to understand further is also a key part of deep listening.

Take note that deep listening requires a "present moment" practice that you will read more about in the next section, on spirit. In each moment of listening, you are practicing staying present with each word that is being said and with the idea that is formulated by the words you are hearing. Even as the idea comes together, you continue to follow the flow of the speaker from word to word, thought to thought. As a deep listener, your goal is to fully receive and understand the entirety of what the speaker is saying to you. Be aware of your mind wanting to grab a hold of a particular point or idea and wanting to react with a judgment or opinion. Judging is not a part of deep listening.

HAPPINESS SKILLS AND PRACTICES

Being a Deep Listener

You can practice deep listening by tuning into podcasts, recorded books, or streaming presentations online such as TED Talks. The benefit of this practice is that, because there is not a speaker present, you have time and space to practice and notice the following:

- Am I getting distracted by outside noises or happenings?
- Am I losing track of what's being said because I'm focusing on a point that was already made?
- Am I thinking about anything other than what I am hearing?

When you notice that you have stayed in one spot while the speaker has moved ahead or that you were perhaps distracted and lost track altogether, rewind to where you left off, pause there, note any idea you want to come back to, and continue listening from there with the goal of staying present with the speaker, word by word, thought by thought. Once you feel confident with this practice, take it live with people in your workplace, your home, and other aspects of the world around you. This is especially important with the people closest to you, so be sure to practice at home.

Deep listening is a mindfulness practice, which means your mind is full of that which is in the present moment. If speaking a word takes one second, then in deep listening during that second, your mind is on that word. In the next second, it is on the next word, and so on.

Perfecting your deep listening skills takes time! Every time you do this well, celebrate! When you notice you have lost track in a conversation or drifted away, become present with the word the person is saying at that moment and reconnect with your present moment.

Well done!

BEING FLEXIBLE

Being flexible is a practice that benefits those around you and helps keep your heart open and confident. Being flexible can be as simple as taking a pause when a child needs your attention or saying "yes" to a different vacation than the one you had researched so meticulously. This is a good practice for both large and small situations.

Being flexible is made possible by a deep, abiding confidence and trust that all will be well. Allowing change is also about letting go of the outcome you had originally envisioned and allowing a new and different one to emerge. It's the difference between being open to opportunity and having tunnel vision. When you're flexible, you realize that life is not so much about right decisions and wrong decisions. Rather a life lived in fullness comes from being open to the new, to possibility, to change, to learning, and to growing.

Perhaps you plan a wonderful trip with a beautifully detailed itinerary. Imagine you meet some fascinating local people in a place you are visiting. They offer to take you on an amazing personal tour of their area the next day, seeing things you wouldn't see any other way. Of course, you already have the next day planned. Do you seize the opportunity to see things you otherwise would have missed? Or is it too hard for you to let go of what you've already planned?

Being flexible is just as important in small ways, such as going down a street you've never been on as you go to the store or even just folding your towel in a new way.

HAPPINESS SKILLS AND PRACTICES

Learning to Be Flexible

Specific areas to notice in assessing your own flexibility are as follows:

Letting go of control of a situation

Compromise

Accepting change

Trying new things

The confidence to do all of the above

As with other happiness skills, first take time to observe yourself in terms of being flexible. Make journal notes about what you're noticing.

- Are you rigid when considering new options when you've already made a plan?

- Are you open to new possibilities?

- Are you happy and willing to try new things?

- Are you willing to compromise with others when planning and making decisions?

- Notice what's happening in your body at these times. Does your jaw tighten, do your shoulders tense, does your stomach tighten?

Evolving your awareness may be enough to bring your attention to any changes and to guide you as you fine-tune yourself to be more open and more flexible. Remember your skills from the Body section—grounding, movement, breathing. Lots of deep breathing!

You can practice flexibility by setting an intention to do the following (You may want to review the "Setting Intention" part of the Mind 3 chapter.):

- Change a plan one time each week.

- Let someone else make a plan when you normally would, and be gracious about going along with it.

- Change a pattern such as the route you drive home each day, the order in which you go through your morning routine, or the place you sit to watch TV or read.

- Say yes to something you would normally say no to. This could be having a cup of coffee with a friend, doing something with a child, or going for a walk when you would normally sit and read. You might try listening to different music and even going out to dance!

- Do yoga regularly and often. This is the literal embodiment of flexibility. This handbook is written to address happiness through mind, body, heart, and spirit. Though we look at them separately, they all work together as one being, you! As you feel flexibility in your body with yoga, a sense of ease and release will pass through your whole being. With that comes the sense that being flexible is joyful and is a subtle encouragement to practice it.

If you have traditionally been rigid rather than flexible, keep going as you practice flexibility in baby steps. You will find more joy as you allow for new things, share your choices with others, and make people in your life a priority in this way. Accepting change with ease is a mega happiness skill!

As with all the happiness skills, choosing is a key part of this. Choosing to be flexible will increase your happiness! Of course, it may feel challenging at first. If so, just go one step at a time. If you are already a flexibility master, yay for you!

YOU CAN ONLY CONTROL YOU

This is a phrase I use often in coaching. We may try to control children and spouses, even parents or employees. Doing so creates drama, tension, and havoc in relationships. We want people to make what we think are best choices, which is our belief interfering with the autonomy of others. Controlling behavior takes away from good relationships and satisfying interactions with others. Unless there is an agreement in place where two people have agreed to give and accept guidance, such as a teacher and a student, then your suggestions and advice should not be offered unless asked for. No one wants to be told what to do. Our resistance to this begins as infants and often becomes more pronounced as we age. Giving unsolicited advice is not a good choice.

This happiness skill calls for you to take care of living your best life through your choices for yourself, accepting that the people around you also have the same right. This can be hard, I know. People you love may be in crisis, and you may see clearly what you believe will help them. For example, you may be in a loving relationship with an alcoholic or drug addict. You don't understand why they don't just quit, or at least get help, but telling them that will not make it so. Only they can make that choice.

This is the other person's life, journey, and choices. Your advice and guidance will only be heard if it's asked for; if the person asks for your help, then you can choose to help. If the person does not want your input, then you can only control yourself and the choices you make.

If a friend is sharing with you about difficulties at work or in a relationship, this is a good time to practice your skill of listening. People want to be heard and will frequently shut down if you respond with advice or opinions. If there's something you want to say, it works well to ask, "Would you like my input, or would you prefer I just listen?" Then accept that person's answer with ease and hold that listening space for him or her. If for some reason this listening is hard for you, it's fine to set a boundary and bring the conversation to a close.

You can only control you, your choices, and your well- being.

HAPPINESS SKILLS AND PRACTICE

Self-awareness

Self-awareness is the skill to practice with this. Notice when you are about to tell someone what to do. Instead of saying anything, practice deep listening.

For example, you may have a friend telling you about her husband having an affair. You want to jump in with an "I told you so" and advice to leave him.

Try this instead: Simply listen quietly. If she asks what you think, begin with sympathetic comments about how you can hear that she's suffering. You can support her by asking her what she thinks and what she needs to do now to support herself.

Learning to support people this way is a great gift to you and to them. People will have their own best answers inside of themselves. What they need is someone to ask, "What do you think you should do?" or "What would help you with this?" This is reflecting their questions back to them. This can go on through a whole conversation and may take time. Time to talk out their thoughts and feelings is what people often need rather than the well-meaning input of others. This is an important place for deep listening.

If the other person persists in asking what you think and asking for your advice, go easy. Remember, a heavy emotional download of your thoughts and opinions will distract the person from the process of getting to his or her own best answers.

Repeat your remarks of support and compassion: "I can see how you're hurting. I'm so sorry for what you're going through. I believe your answers will come. Let some time pass and see what comes clear for you then. What can you do right now to take care of yourself? I know it's hard, and yet you can only control your next steps and taking care of yourself."

If you decide to share any of your thoughts, a good technique you can use is to make "I" statements.

For example, you could say, "I think I would do _____ or _____. If I were in this situation, I might_____." Then pause and let them think things through. Remind them that what's right for them will be unique to them, and to their situation.

Quiet pauses in a conversation often make people uneasy, and yet this can be the most important part of communication. Allowing time for the listener to process what's been said is important and a great skill. Practice being comfortable with quiet, extended pauses in conversations. Do not rush to fill them with words that distract from what's been shared and is then being thought through.

As you practice the concept that you can only control you, you will notice increased ease in letting go. It's freeing to bring the focus to living your own best self and giving space to others to do the same. We can listen, love, and support, yet we cannot fix or live other people's lives for them. Boundaries are necessary to honor one another this way. Letting go of trying to get people to listen to you and do what you think they should do is a necessary step. Practice this, and see your relationships change for the better.

Summary

The things I commit to doing

Check the yellow box for each Skill and Practice you are saying 'yes' to. ✔

☐ *Being Aware of Your Accomplishments*

☐ *Being a Deep Listener*

☐ *Learning to Be Flexible*

☐ *Self-Awareness*

Do you want to create reminders for any of these?

HEART 5

A Handbook for LIFE 169

Heart Happiness Skills Summary

Would you like to highlight the ones you are saying yes to?

SELF-LOVE

What Do You Value about You?

Being Your Own Best Friend

Self-Nurture, Self-Care

Cultivating Self-Love

Connecting with Your Younger Self

Fun Alone Time with You!

How Are You Doing Loving Yourself?

THE POWER OF CONNECTION

Connect!

Relationship Boundaries

Observe Yourself

Journal Your Observations

GIVING AND RECEIVING

Make a Commitment to Give

Set Your Intention to Give

Notice Your Feelings

Set Your Intention to Receive

Ask for What You Need

Saying Yes and Saying No

GRATITUDE IS AMAZING

Think Grateful Thoughts

Embody Gratitude

Write It Down: Your Gratitude Journal

A to Z

Grateful for Things Large and Small

Say It Out Loud

You

BEING YOUR BEST SELF

Being Aware of Your Accomplishments

Being a Deep Listener

Learning to Be Flexible

Self-Awareness

What is spirit? What is spiritual being?

Think of this as you would peaceful being or joyful being. What does it feel like to experience spiritual being? How does spirit impact us, who we are, and how we live?

Your spirit is the part of you that is your true self. That which filled our little embryonic bodies to activate the person who lives here is our spirit. Your spirit landed in a human physical embryo that grew into your body, and as your spirit settled into your human state, you were born, you lived, and you evolved your heart and mind. All of this is who you are, and it all began with your spirit, and it's your spirit that makes you you. Being in touch with and living from your core, your spirit, is the point of the Happiness Is a Skill work.

As the foundation of our being, that which is most truly who we are, spirit is naturally balanced. When we let go of all the noise in our heads and our hearts, when we get quiet enough to settle into our spiritual selves that live in the core of us, we find balance there.

There is much written about the separation between spirit and ego. The concept is that the ego is more of a human creation, built on the construct of judgment. From ego thinking comes measuring the worth of a person (including yourself), that person's value, and how "good" or "bad" that person is in any given measure that the ego uses.

When coming from the perspective of spirit, there is no judgment because love sits at its foundation, and love does not judge. This use of the word "spirit" is not connected to a dogmatic religion, which is another system for measuring and rulemaking. Spirit is simply the energy that imbues your human body with life. When your body ceases to live, your spirit goes on.

Sometimes you hear the word "spirit" used as a reference for God, the universe, higher power, and so on. Other times you hear it as a reference to a member of the Holy Trinity in Christianity, the Holy Spirit.

For our purposes here, "spirit" refers to you, the essence of you, the core of you, the "who you are" of you. Your spirit refers to the energy that is you. Once your body is done, your spirit "passes over" or "passes on" to whatever is there that we can't see.

Spirit is the calm behind your personal storm of emotions, behind the intellectual brain clutter that gets noisy, behind the endless chatter about "shoulds" and "can'ts" and "should haves."

Your spirit waits patiently for you to notice that calm is good for you and offers serenity whenever you get quiet enough to be there. Happiness is a Skill work is about quieting the human mind and allowing our spirit to filter for what we truly need and what's good for us and to let the rest go.

Wayne Dyer, in his book Wisdom of the Ages, referenced spirit as the sacred self that is, "Inclined to being peaceful, noncompetitive, nonjudgmental, and it never makes demands."

Now that's a pretty great friend to have! That friend lives inside of you and, in fact, is you. During those times when you daydream or meditate, you notice the calm and peaceful release that comes with letting go of the thinking mind and allowing your spirit to be present.

Let's look at how to regularly connect with your spirit.

Intuition is the voice of your spirit. You may believe that God, your higher power, the universe, or whatever else you might call it is the something that is talking to you through your intuition. As it happens, that's right. This can also be thought of as hearing your inner voice, your inner wisdom. Your spirit is the communication platform that connects with all manifestations of a higher power and your higher self. It is your direct connection to wisdom and guidance, and it's available twenty-four seven! Learning to get quiet and access that connection is part of meditating; and for some people it's prayer. None of the words really matter, though. What matters is that you understand that this connection is available and to know that to hear such guidance, a quiet mind and heart are important.

HOW INTUITION WORKS

This begins with

THE UNIVERSE

a higher power or your inner wisdom to

YOUR SPIRIT

then conveyed through

YOUR INTUITION

to your awareness/mind, but only if your mind is quiet and you're available to receive/hear it

Your spirit and your body communicate with each other. Just as your spirit can be activated by your body, so too your body receives messages from your spirit in the form of physical sensations that communicate with you. This is your intuition talking to you, through your body.

Often you'll feel something in your gut and you'll say, "I knew it in my gut." The saying "gut instinct" refers to intuition. Maybe you've said yes to an invitation, but it didn't "feel" right. That's your intuition talking. Have you ever said, "I knew that was going to happen"? This can be intuition too. Intuition is one way you will hear the guidance that is always available to you. Practice noticing these voices and trusting what you hear.

You will have guidance that shows up in your journaling. With practice, having a direct connection to intuition and guidance through your spirit becomes normal and easy as you continue practicing all of your happiness skills. This is one of the great gifts of this work since life becomes much easier when you listen to and follow your intuition and spiritual guidance.

HAPPINESS SKILLS AND PRACTICES

Each of these skills and practices is presented in other areas of the handbook, and the skills are important in your reading here as well.

Meditation

Meditation is a practice of quieting your mind. It is a wonderful way to get right into the heart and soul of yourself, your spirit. As you quiet your mind, that sweet voice of knowing, of guidance, and of slow, easy processing can be heard.

In the next section, you will be given much more on meditation, including how to meditate. Choose to practice meditation daily, and you'll begin developing the quiet you need to hear your guidance.

Body Voices

Think back to Body Voices chapter 3 in the Body section. The choice you make now is to develop your awareness of your body through meditation. Your big toe hurts? What's there? Your lower back is acting up? What's there? There's a wonderful book from Louise Hay called You Can Heal Your Life. In the back of that book is an alphabetical listing of things that show up in your body and what they indicate. This list became a very important reference that helped me learn what symptoms our bodies may produce and what those symptoms may be telling us. My understanding evolved as I journaled about my particular set of body voices and what they meant in my life.

With this information, you will begin to learn to understand your own body and what it feels. You can make better choices about your happiness, your peace, and your well-being as you increase this awareness. As you observe your body and its sensations, write in your journal what you feel and notice, what is going on at that time, and all the details that you perceive. You will begin to see patterns and connections between your body aches, pains, tingles, and twitches and other things happening in your life.

Let me give you one example. I had a client who for years each morning had felt an odd pain in her lower back that went around to her lower abdominal area. She would stand there at the sink, rubbing her lower back as she tended to her family's needs, including getting the kids off to school. She was also in chronic emotional pain in her marriage, not feeling safe to express her mounting emotional turmoil. She had a lot of personal, emotional work to do. Once she began to unload that pain and make changes in herself to create a more resonant life, the lower-body morning pains disappeared.

Journaling

Journaling allows you to "hear" what your intuition wants you to know. Letting go of the outcome of your writing and letting go of thought and simply putting pen to paper and keeping your hand moving can reveal much to you that might otherwise be elusive. Your spirit has a lot to share through your journaling.

Hopefully you have been journaling since you first read about it in the introduction. If you missed that, please read it now. With consistent journaling your connection to your spiritual knowing will become stronger, and your writing will become clearer and more helpful to you.

Summary

The things I commit to doing

Check the yellow box for each Skill and Practice you are saying 'yes' to. ✔

 Meditation

 Body Voices

 Journaling

Do you want to create reminders for any of these?

Connecting with Spirit: Meditation, Peace, and Balance

With a quiet mind, so much more is possible as you create the life you want. Your quiet mind is the foundation for your happy, fulfilling life.

When we connect with our spiritual self, ever present in our core, both peace and balance are immediately available.

Think about that for a minute.

You are walking around twenty-four seven with peace and balance right inside of you, immediately available—once you practice connecting with it. That's an incredible, life-changing resource, and you can have instant access to it!

The supercool thing about connecting to your spiritual self is this: Each time you connect with the serenity and peace there, your spirit is further energized. You expand the reservoir of all that comes to you from this place. The balance, peace, serenity, and so much more. Your inner voice of knowing and of innate wisdom becomes easier to hear as you get quiet and connect deeply inside of you.

All forms of quieting your mind lead to this place. Seated meditation is the primary practice for this. Practicing the things you love to do can also clear the clutter of other noise from your head and allow you to drop down into your body, which is the first step in connecting with your spiritual self.

When you are absorbed in something fulfilling, your mind quiets and your inner voice can be heard. Perhaps you're a bicyclist out on the open road; your head quiets and your deeper self comes forward. Maybe you're a rower and as you move those oars back and forth, working deeply in your body, you have an epiphany about something you've been stuck on. The point is that when you are fully focused on something absorbing, your mind quiets, which opens the pathway to deeper knowing—to hearing your guidance. Using and moving your body also contributes to this process.

Let me add here that the experience of connecting with your spiritual self is for some people characterized by a feeling of connecting with "God," a higher power, the source, and a variety of other concepts all addressing the same thing.

As you live your life in harmony with your spirit, you live with balance and peace. That's the bottom line to this. It's also the reason to practice meditation often—to access this amazing resource.

MEDITATION

Many practices help you to get out of your head and into your spirit. Daily prayer, journaling, meditation, chanting, dancing, movement, having fun—you name it! What's yours? Maybe it's creating your art, singing, music, or handicrafts. The things that deeply fulfill you are in fact filling your spirit, and you are present from that place of your spirit.

The power of meditation to fulfill this function cannot be overstated. Meditation is the foundation for "hearing" your wisdom and guidance, for accessing peace, balance, and ease. How can you possibly say no to all of that?

Meditation is simply a quieting of your mind. That's all. Nothing fancy, nothing hard, nothing complicated. It takes commitment to practice consistently. That may be the hardest part. Our minds are accustomed to being busy and noisy. As you begin practicing meditation, your mind will need some time to understand that what you want it to do is different from what you have been wanting it to do before.

If you have been busy with your phone and computer, family and work, friends and all the details of living, then you may not have ever asked your mind to be quiet. So allow time for this shift to occur. It's a slow, progressive change. It will take however long it takes, and you will get to the point of deeply quiet meditation only with persistence and practice.

Meditation allows us to retrain our brains. In meditation it's OK to let go of thinking. In fact, it's the whole point. You remain aware, yet it's inside a quiet, gentle mind, cultivated with practice. This is not a chance for sleeping, so if you find yourself falling asleep, gently tell yourself to come back.

I'm going to take one segue here into the physical aspect of how meditation works to improve your happiness. Simply said, meditation creates a healthier brain. During meditation, your billions of neurons that are continuously sending neurotransmitters out to receptors increase production of good chemicals such as serotonin, DHEA, GABA, human growth hormone, and melatonin. Those chemicals are major players that do the following for you:

- Give you a sense of well being

- Increase longevity

- Increase a feeling of calm

- Increase feeling good, happy

- Decrease pain

- Revive tissues in your body promoting health

- Promote more restful sleep

Additionally, meditation has been shown to reduce the production of cortisol. Chronic cortisol production is a consequence of stress. This can promote weight gain, anxiety, depression, increased blood pressure, brain fog, insomnia, and inflammation. So if you needed a more tangible reason to meditate, there you go.

There are numerous apps to teach you about meditation and to support your meditation practice, including recordings of guided mediations that encourage your mind to be present and quiet. This guidance can really help you learn how to let go and calm your mind. Guided meditation can be very helpful if sitting quietly on your own doesn't work for you. Some apps will give you calming background sounds and music. This can give your mind something to attach to other than the thoughts that keep wanting to come through.

While there are benefits available from guided meditation and it can be a good place to begin, I believe the goal is to meditate simply and with yourself, cultivating a fully quiet mind. Your mind is not truly going to achieve quiet as it listens to words of guidance suggesting what to think about.

HAPPINESS SKILLS AND PRACTICES

Meditation: "Keep coming back"

Essentially, all you need to meditate are these factors:

1. The desire to meditate

2. A calm, quiet, comfortable place to sit

3. A commitment to sit comfortably (I find lying down promotes going to sleep—not what we're after). You may want to use a pillow or cushion to sit on. You can also meditate sitting on a chair or sofa, in your car, on an airplane—anywhere quiet, really.

It's just this easy. It's committing to being consistent that is the big step for many people. How about you? Are you ready to consistently practice meditating each day?

It's very helpful to set your phone timer or use an app timer so that you are not wondering how long you've been meditating. I like Insight Timer, which has many gongs and bells that you can choose to sound along with the beginning and ending timer. And it has lovely background music and sounds. Also included are guided meditations. You can find it at **insighttimer.com**.

You'll start with a short time, perhaps five to ten minutes, and increase the time as you go. Set a goal for yourself, maybe thirty, forty-five, or sixty minutes.

I have several clients who have a special meditation place they've created in their homes. It may have their favorite chair, meditation cushion, candles, some incense, and special objects—totems and things they've gathered to enhance the sense of peace in their space.

How to Meditate: The Basics

Seat yourself comfortably in a quiet space where you will not be interrupted.

If there are any wiggles that need to come out, or you're uncomfortable in any way, let all of that out and settle back in.

If you are using an audio assist such as a timer or guided meditation, turn that on.

- Close your eyes.
- Breathe in deeply, with ease.
- Breathe out completely, again with ease.
- The mouth can be open or closed, whichever you prefer.
- Continue this breathing pattern as you meditate.

Release any tightness in trigger points in your body such as the jaw, shoulders, chest, stomach, hips, thighs, or knees.

Allow your mind to drift, with the eventual goal of complete quieting.

As thoughts come through your mind, simply let them go rather than focusing in and pursuing them.

For example, you might think, "Oh, I forgot to take out the trash."

Let that go, knowing that anything you think of during meditation will be there when you're done.

Come back and anchor by noticing your breath.

You can also anchor to sounds you hear. This might be distant traffic noises, the sound of the refrigerator, or a dog barking somewhere. Keep coming back to this place if your mind wanders.

- Come back to your breath.

- Come back to sounds you hear.

- Anchor your practice and come back.

- Keep coming back.

When the timer goes off at the end of your session, and when you're ready, slowly open your eyes, first looking down and pausing there. Slowly move your hands and your feet, to awaken your body gently.

Allow your mind to readjust to the present moment.

Great job! Whatever happened, you did it! Each meditation brings its own value and is "just right." Celebrate yourself. It's called a meditation "practice" for a reason.

As you plan your meditation practice, think about these questions: Where will you meditate? Do you want to download Insight Timer or another app? How often and how long will you meditate? As you answer these questions and begin to see your next steps, put the time you're committing to meditation in your planner and begin. Simply showing up and sitting is enough. Whether your mind wanders is not the point. The point is to begin and keep coming back with the intention to become calmer and quieter in your mind, one day at a time. Each time is perfect as it is. Trust that. Meditation is for a lifetime, and now you've begun.

Well done!

A note here about meditation cushions: It can be fun and very comfortable to have the cushions that are made for sitting on the floor. You can check out meditation supply websites for specialty items such as zafus (cushions) and zabutons (mats).

My Meditation Story

For me, learning to meditate was a practice in "keeping it simple." I had a yoga instructor who began class by saying, "Quiet your chattering mind," and I got that. My mind was always looking for a topic to chatter on about. In fact, I had spent years keeping a mental list of things that I needed to worry about. It was normal for me.

So that's where I was as I began seated meditation. I'm using "seated" literally. I might have been seated in my car, on a bench outside, or in a yoga pose. I started by taking two or three minutes and checking in with my chattering mind to see if I could allow for a couple of minutes of quieting. As soon as I did this, my mind slowed down. The thoughts I was having seemed like a movie running in front of my eyes, and I slowly stopped engaging with the story line and let the story run on by.

It was cool.

Even better was that I found that I actually liked the peace I felt and wanted more. I kind of felt like a junkie. Surrendering my worry was awesome!

With practice came the gift of being able to drop into deep quiet in a moment, anytime, anywhere. As I grew and evolved myself and this program of Happiness Is a Skill, my brain completely changed. Meditation was the foundation for that. It is a major foundational happiness skill, for sure!

Creating Resonance for Connecting with Your Spirit

This section would not be complete without encouraging you to do the things you love, which creates peacefulness inside of you. That peacefulness allows for your inner knowing, your higher power, your spirit to come through. As you labor over a lump of clay or pedal hard up a hill, you are in resonance and harmony with your spirit. In moments like that, you are open and available to receive thoughts that may seem random, and yet you find those thoughts are answers to a question or solutions to a problem you have been working on.

So what do you love to do? Write about those things here. Include what it is about those things that you love and how you feel doing them. As you design your life around happiness skills, choose to spend more time with the things you list here. Put them in your planner.

I love to do the following:

_____

_____

_____

_____

_____

_____

_____

_____

_____

_____

_____

_____

_____

_____

Summary

The things I commit to doing

Check the yellow box for each Skill and Practice you are saying 'yes' to.

 Meditation

Creating Resonance for Connecting with Your Spirit

Do you want to create reminders for any of these?

"Be where your feet are." These often-used words are a good mantra to keep you present.

Mindfulness means that your mind is fully present and filled by the moment you are in right now.

Let's look at an example. You are out for a walk and you are noticing where your feet are, where you're putting them. Is there a pothole there or a puddle? Are you stepping around that or through that? Is there traffic, or are there people in your space? You are aware of what's in that moment. You are fully present.

Let's look at another example. A mother is getting her kids in the car to go to school. She is fully present with that moment as she notices whether their seat belts are on, and she checks to see if they have their backpacks and lunches. She does not have an awareness of the time in terms of being late or on time. She is simply in that moment of mindfully getting everyone in the car safely and with everything they need.

As she leaves the driveway and begins the drive to school, she focuses fully in each moment of driving. She knows everything that is around her, including where the other cars are. She is noticing the changes in their location in relationship to her car; she is noticing the signs and the stoplights. Her mind is fully in that moment, one moment to the next, as she drives safely to school.

As she drives, the kids begin to fuss and get unhappy with each other. Here is a great opportunity to notice that she chooses to be mindful. This choice is in her present moment and she chooses to be fully present.

Part of being fully present is evolving a filter for what supports and what diminishes our presence. Let me repeat that. Part of being fully present is evolving a filter for what supports and what diminishes our presence. Choosing what to allow into our consciousness is the act of filtering.

In this case, if the kids begin to get loud and angry, this mom is at a choice point. With her filter activated to be mindfully present, she chooses to stay fully focused on the road and the cars around her. This is what it is to be truly mindful.

If the kids become very distracting and her filter is challenged, then her mindfulness enables her to stay focused on the driving while looking for a safe way to pull over. As she does that, staying very present and focused, she comes to a stop and parks. Now she turns mindfully to the children and addresses their situation.

As you practice mindfulness and incorporate being fully present into your life, you will notice that you become calmer. Let's look at that in the example of driving the kids.

The woman's mindfulness filter kept her fully present and focused on the driving. She was separate from the kids and their conflict. She stayed present with her breathing, keeping her eyes on the road and aware of her surroundings. To support her mindful presence, she needed to consciously release any tension in her body. She kept her ears tuned to driving noises and not children's voices. She was fully present with the things that were the most important in each moment, by choice. She was calm because she was taking only one moment at a time, which felt manageable and promoted calm.

Had she become engaged in the kids' problems while she was driving, answering them when they said, "Mom, Tommy took my lunch box," she would not then have been fully present with driving, and that would have put all of them at risk.

We are responsible for what we choose to allow into each moment. That sounds like a big statement, and it is. If someone is yelling at you, mindful presence teaches you that you make a choice in that moment about how you respond to the yelling. Noticing the yelling is one moment. Choosing what you will do is the next moment, then taking that action is the next moment. Mindfulness enables you to focus down to small, manageable moments. It's a pretty great tool.

No one makes or forces anyone to do anything. We may respond to some stimulus from another person, such as the fighting children in the back seat, but that moment of choice belongs to us, not the person wanting our attention. We choose where we put our attention, and being aware of that choice is the key to living mindfully.

So, mindfulness is comprised of these factors:

- Focusing on the present moment

- Choosing our response to what is there

- Practicing tools that support our presence

HAPPINESS SKILLS AND PRACTICES

Several of these skills and practices are covered in other places in the handbook. I am including them again here as they are so key to mindfulness and presence. I suggest you read them again here since the wording is a bit different.

Meditation

Meditation is the best practice and skill for cultivating focus, which supports presence by paying attention to what is. A quiet mind more easily sees what's there, concentrates and is clearer when making choices. Since you can read about that in the previous section and plan for your meditation practice, let's look at some other skills and practices for mindful presence.

Movement

Body movement brings you into the present moment. If you are sitting at your computer and your mind is wandering, get up and walk, bend, twist, or do some yoga. Move. Any movement will shift you from distraction to presence. Movement engages your mind and brings it to presence.

Try it now. Stand up and reach for the sky. Hold that for a moment, then bend fully at the waist toward the ground. Hang out there for a minute or two. Twist, swing your arms, play with the posture. You will become present as you notice the sensations in your muscles, the feelings in your body as you bend and reach. Bring your torso back up and reach for the sky. Now you are present with your body.

Walking is always a good way to shift and become present. Even five minutes for a change of scene makes a difference. And drink some water.

You can use any movements that you like in this practice: jumping up and down, tapping (which is a whole other book) your face, arms, and head, scrunching your face, and tightening and releasing muscles. Your body has lots of moving parts, so move them!

The point is to get moving and to give your mind something to be present with. Our bodies are a powerful part of our team and are purveyors of presence.

Now come back to your computer, your mind refreshed and present for the next work session.

Breathing

Breathing deeply and slowly, with a complete in-breath and a full out-breath, focusing on the air going in and going out, is a mindfulness practice. This brings you back to the present moment instantly. Now do that as you release your jaw and drop your shoulders. Breathe, release. Keep coming back to this. It's an instant reset to bring you back to being present.

Settling into the Earth

Stand in Mountain Pose, feet hip-width apart.

Breathe in deeply, and as you breathe out, release your trigger points, beginning with your neck, jaw, shoulders, arms, stomach, hips, thighs, knees, ankles, and down through your feet. Release your weight fully into the earth, feeling solidly grounded in your feet. Feel your solid connection to the earth under your feet. This gives you support, grounds you, holds you.

Listening with Presence

If you find yourself drifting while listening to someone speak and not being present, focus on each sentence that person is saying. Stay with the person, word for word. Do not attach any thought or form opinions as the person speaks. Rather, listen to the words with the intention of fully understanding the meaning. Do this listening as though you were learning a foreign language. You would be listening intently for the words you know and focusing on understanding what the foreign language speaker was saying. That would be bringing presence to listening.

Pausing for Presence

Choosing your response in the present moment is part of the whole body of work of happiness skills. As you cultivate a calm heart, mind, body, and spirit, you are more naturally able to pause in any moment to choose your response. This pause may only take seconds. What it allows is space to choose your next action rather than having a reaction. Taking action from choice is a mindful practice while reacting without thinking and assessing is a mindless reaction.

In our world, planning and thinking ahead are necessary. We plan our children's activities and family activities, our travels, doctor appointments, and more. We do these things being fully present with the process we are in. If you are an attorney and planning a case you are taking to court in the future, you are mindfully in the present moment of preparation. So, yes, it is possible to live in the present moment fully while tending to the real-life chores of past and future.

If you operate a small business and you are doing your projections for next year's sales and expenses, you are mindful of that process in the present moment. You use all of the skills and practices to bring your mindful presence to that task.

If you get into a difficult conversation with someone about past events, including perceived wrongs and hurts, then you use mindfulness to bring that conversation into the present. You pause to sort out what's there at that moment. You mindfully listen and hear that there may be hurt feelings, even anger, based on beliefs about past events. The events are in the past, and the feelings are in the present. With your mindful presence, you see what's there at the time that needs loving kindness, acknowledgment, and attention. You talk about this from the perspective of being in the present moment, what's there at the moment, rather than what's past. The healing that's being asked for is in the present, not the past.

It may be necessary to take a pause, which allows for time to slow emotions and change the momentum, then calmly share what's possible for you from there. You will be breathing, releasing trigger points, dropping your weight through the bottom of your feet into the earth. If the other person, or people, are not able to engage with you mindfully, then you will make the choice that best serves your well-being at that moment.

Let me offer an example: You are having a conversation with a family member who you are not very close to. This person is expressing anger that you did not include him or her in a family event sometime in the past. It takes you a minute to remember what this person is talking about, and as you listen, the voice of the family member begins to rise, and the words come faster. The negative emotions are gaining momentum.

You notice your cheeks begin to flush, a sign that this person's energy is creating an impact on yours. You mindfully choose to breathe slowly and allow for a pause, taking several slow, deep breaths as the angry comments come to an end. You choose to keep a soft expression on your face and comment that you can see how this is upsetting to the family member. When you are fully present in your body, you respond:

"I'm so sorry you are feeling upset. As I remember this now, the only people at the event were my immediate family and not the extended family."

This person may continue the angry spiral and have another comeback for you. At that point, with a calming breath and pause as the person speaks, you can reiterate that you're sorry the person is having these hard feelings and that it was not personal. You can stress that you are together there and then, and that it's nice to have that happen. Smile, breathe, and move on. That is mindfully bringing a conversation about the past into the present. As you leave that conversation, it stays in the moment that is then past, and you walk into the next present moment.

As you practice being present and mindful, create a good moment and repeat, repeat, repeat!

Summary

The things I commit to doing

Check the yellow box for each Skill and Practice you are saying 'yes' to. ☑

☐ *Meditation*

☐ *Movement*

☐ *Breathing*

☐ *Settling into the Earth*

☐ *Listening with Presence*

☐ *Pausing for Presence*

Do you want to create reminders for any of these?

Curiosity, creativity, and courage are spirit in action. Passion too. When you get passionately excited about something, that is your spirit saying yes!

Spirit in Action: Curiosity, Creativity, Courage, and Passion

Do that, go there, make that happen. Yes to being creative! Yes to curiosity and pursuing meaningful, fulfilling ideas, projects, and goals! This is where courage comes in. Saying yes to something often takes courage. Looking into the unknown, doing something you've never done before, going beyond what's familiar—all this takes courage. When curiosity leads you to discover and to learn, this is your spirit in action, guiding you and saying "yes." Trust that.

Creativity and curiosity are forms of energy, and as such, they have momentum. Following them takes being just a little braver than you are afraid, so you step up and say "yes!"—I'll do this thing that seems crazy or that thing that I've never tried. When you apply this to giving, to sharing, or to showing up in the world as you, you're living your best life.

 One way I live my creativity is by writing what you're reading right now. Some days it's superhard for me to sit here and type, but my inner guidance says, "Keep going; this is the right thing to be doing now." So I do. I'm creating something that feels important to me to share, and when the timer goes off (Yep, I have to set a timer to keep myself mindfully focused!), I feel fulfilled, knowing that I'm following my inner guidance. This, in turn, keeps me coming back to this work. I trust this guidance, and I know that as I stay in each present moment, I'll go exactly where I'm intended to go and do what I'm intended to do.

The thing you are doing, your creative idea or project, only has to feel important to you. This is not about what anyone else thinks; this is only about what you feel and what your intuition is telling you to do. You're the only one in your way with the negative self-talk. So get out of the way; stop the negative self-talk, be brave, and sign up for that class. You may not be creating something you love until you get some lessons. That's OK. Having creativity doesn't mean you are naturally gifted as a macramé weaver. It means you are brave enough to learn and practice and try because you secretly want to. It means you are curious about how it works and about what you can make. Let that secret longing out! Go for it!

When you twirl around your living room just because it feels good in your body, you're being creative. Maybe you're also curious about how many turns you can do and not fall over. These two energies sync up to lead you to more life, more fulfillment, more fun, and more passionate living.

When you're curious if you can back your car into the garage at a certain angle, you're being creative and satisfying your curiosity. Creativity is as simple or as complex as you want to make it. No matter what, though, creative living brings more happiness into your life. So, hey, creative self, muster your courage and curiosity and come on out.

I have a friend who is super creative with how she brushes her teeth. She makes it fun for herself and her kids by asking them, "How many times can you brush your teeth on the top today? How about the bottom?" She gets them curious, then brings in creativity as she lets them go outside and use a pan of water to swoosh and rinse.

Then there's the neighbor who arranges his flowerpots in a heart shape to share love with the world. That's his spirit talking. Let yourself flow from your spirit, from who you truly are, and be curious about what comes. It's a new day. Let's see this in a new way.

Our spirits want us to be fulfilled, to live a life of meaning. Fulfillment is a spiritual response to doing things that fill us deeply. This is happiness, and wherein lies that happiness is a spiritual response. This is why we have curiosity, creativity, and courage. Together they lead us to discovering what fuels our passions and how to live a fulfilled life.

HAPPINESS SKILLS AND PRACTICES

These exercises are designed to bring together your curiosity, creativity, courage, and passion to lead you into a deeply fulfilling, happy life.

What Lights Your Fire?

What topic lights your fire, gets your juices flowing? What are you passionate about? Saving the planet, respecting animal rights, teaching meditation in schools? Maybe you are passionate about science, religion, or art. What are the things that really light you up when you're talking to friends or reading articles online? What are the things that excite you?

1. _____

_____

_____

2. _____

_____

_____

3.   _____

_____

_____

4.   _____

_____

_____

5.   _____

_____

_____

6.   _____

_____

_____

More? Add those too.

Write why you are passionate about each of these things. Why is this important to you? What intrigues you, triggers your interest and caring? Be detailed, and remember, this is just for you, so be open, honest, and real, and remember that there's no editing of yourself. Let it flow.

1.   _____

_____

_____

2. _____

_____

_____

3. _____

_____

_____

4. _____

_____

_____

5. _____

_____

_____

6. _____

_____

_____

What comes up as you think and write about your passions? What's here that you want to pursue? Write in detail as you answer these.

_____

_____

_____

_____

_____

_____

_____

_____

_____

_____

_____

_____

_____

_____

_____

_____

_____

When you've completed this, check what you've written for any action you'd like to take on your topics and interests. Maybe it's research, and you want to know more, or possibly you're ready for something more concrete. Use the process in Mind 5, Moving Forward Fearlessly, for setting your goals, writing your intention for each, and the planning action steps. Then put those steps in your planner and get going!

Your Unattended Longings

What have you secretly longed to learn, to try, or do? You know, the thing that pops in your mind now and then that you dismiss, thinking of every reason it's not practical or possible?

Well, that's old thinking, and now you are living by your happiness skills, so let's go there! Maybe it's line dancing, painting, or flying. Have you secretly wanted to learn about computer code or meteorology? Perhaps you simply want to try painting a room in your home or making a scrapbook for a friend. What ideas have you had that you've been afraid to try or you've been putting off until "someday"?

This list is just for you. Write anything and everything you want to do, learn, try, and know about!

1. _____

_____

_____

2. _____

_____

_____

3. _____

_____

_____

4. _____

_____

_____

5. _____

_____

_____

6. _____

_____

_____

7. _____

_____

_____

8. _____

_____

_____

More? Keep going!

Choose one (or more) to focus on now. Again, refer to Mind 5, Moving Forward Fearlessly, for the process behind making these changes a reality. Let me emphasize the importance of scheduling time in your planners to bring this idea to life! You can do this!

Summary

The things
I commit
to doing

Check the yellow box for each Skill and Practice you are saying 'yes' to.

☐ *What Lights Your Fire?*

☐ *Your Unattended Longings*

Do you want to create reminders for any of these?

Spirit
Nourishment:
Expanding,
Exploring,
Learning,
and Growing

*Expanding, exploring, learning, and growing—
just as our bodies, minds, and hearts need
nourishment, so too does our spirit.*

Our spirits are infinite. As we live this life, we have the opportunity to learn, expand, and grow our spirits through experiences, exploration, reading, and connection with others and with ourselves. We can investigate all we are drawn to know, and trust that we are guided to all the right things. We can set our intention to grow and learn each day, which will move us powerfully to things we are guided to learn. By staying humble and grateful, and being open to the guidance of our spirits, we will live fulfilling lives with a sense of purpose. Breathe that in and feel the ease of this message: "As we stay open and follow the guidance of our spirits, we will live our life of purpose."

That sense of being drawn to know something is your divine guidance in action. Cultivate listening for your guidance, and you will live the life you were meant to live. Quiet and contemplation are necessary in order to listen. Meditation, prayer, working to understand and observe yourself, and journaling all contribute. The processes outlined in Mind 4, the section on curiosity, creativity, and courage, are key to growing your ability to "hear" what is intended for you, what is meant for you in this life. How often do we wonder about the next right step, the right decision to make? Your answers lie in the process and practice of "hearing" your guidance.

I look out the window toward the wonder of the Colorado Rockies, and I see four hummingbirds flitting back and forth on their flight to flower and feeder and back again. They are listening to their guidance. They are finely tuned to their cadence, vibrating through the flight that fulfills their purpose. To nourish, to live, to explore, listening intuitively for the guidance to the next right bush, the next flower. Tending also to the fun of chasing and playing in flight. They are good models for us.

The process of learning happiness skills is a journey in learning about your spirit. As you choose which happiness skills to incorporate into your life, everything in the spirit section of this handbook is foundational to the process. As you work through these skills and practices, you will become intimately familiar with your spirit and come to see yourself from this perspective. You will grow into hearing your inner direction more clearly, and you will naturally become happier. Nourish your spirit as you've read about in this section, and you will optimize the happiness in your life.

HAPPINESS SKILLS AND PRACTICES

The skills and practices from the prior segment apply to this segment, too, with the addition of the following:

Ritual

Throughout this handbook you have been introduced to many practices for expanding your happiness. I have emphasized the importance of consistent and frequent practice to activate your happiness and to bring permanent change in your life. Now I want to add the concept of ritual.

A ritual is a practice that is done regularly, in a particular way, with consistency. It's a pattern. There is something that is so soothing in this form of practice. For example, when you do The Reset, which you learned in the Body 1, The Power of Movement, doing those steps in the same way each time is soothing and nourishing. If you set up a meditation space with candles to light, and you light the candle and approach your sitting in the same way each time as a ritual, you have a deeper, more complete experience. This is ritual. Ritual combines intention and commitment to a certain format that nourishes your practice.

Rituals are particularly nourishing to your spirit. The calming effect of ritual, of knowing something by heart, brings great comfort. In this way, all four aspects of your being are nourished as well. Your body calms, as does your mind and your heart, and your spirit is supported. Ritual is flow and being in flow; it is as calming as a mountain stream. There is a tempo and balance in the sameness, in the predictability, in the known.

As you create rituals—for example, a Morning Pages journaling practice and coffee ritual—bring things you love into it, such as your favorite mug, and of course, your special journal and pen. In meditation you may have a cushion—maybe a zafu that's just right for your seat—some wonderful incense, and objects that are important to you: totems, pictures, daily affirmation cards you have drawn from your deck (see the skills and practices part of the Mind section's chapter 1, What You Think Is What You Create), and anything else you want. These could be arranged on a small table or the floor as you prepare to sit for your meditation, creating a meditation altar of sorts. The time you spend in ritual practice can feel sacred—like a sacred gift to yourself.

How can you apply the concept of ritual to your practice? How can you add in little details and consistency to the way you are doing a particular practice? Write the practice here and describe how you will approach it with detail and consistency.

Practice:

_____

Details I will add:

_____

_____

Practice:

_____

Details I will add:

_____

_____

Practice:

_____

Details I will add:

_____

_____

Practice:

_____

Details I will add:

_____

_____

Practice:

_____

Details I will add:

_____

_____

Now write an intention statement for each idea that you have.

Here's an example: "I intend to set a small table in my sitting room, to place there my little carved bear, pink rose quartz heart, and lavender incense. I will light the incense each time I meditate, sitting on my red zafu. I will do this at the end of each day."

Here's another one: "As I go out the door each morning to walk two miles, I will have my headset and phone with me to listen to soothing music as I walk. I will take the long way around the lake and notice the wildlife there."

And here's another one: "As I write in my journal at bedtime, I will have a cup of chamomile tea and sit in my favorite chair in the study. I will set the timer for fifteen minutes as I wind down to sleep."

Write a statement for each practice you listed:

Practice:

_____

My intention is to:

_____

_____

Practice:

_____

My intention is to:

_____

_____

Practice:

_____

My intention is to:

_____

_____

Practice:

_____

My intention is to:

_____

_____

Practice:

_____

My intention is to:

_____

_____

Follow the intentions you've set and enjoy your happiness skills practices with the soothing influence of ritual. As always, put those intentions in your planner to make them come true!

Well done!

Summary

The things I commit to doing

Check the yellow box for each Skill and Practice you are saying 'yes' to. ☑

 Ritual

Do you want to create reminders for any of these?

Spirit

Happiness

Skills

Summary

Would you like to highlight the ones you are saying yes to?

SPIRIT AND INTUITION

Meditation

Body Voices

Journaling

CONNECTING WITH SPIRIT: MEDITATION, PEACE, AND BALANCE

Meditation

Creating Resonance for Connecting with Your Spirit

MINDFULNESS AND PRESENCE

Meditation

Movement

Breathing

Settling into the Earth

Listening with Presence

Pausing for Presence

SPIRIT IN ACTION: CURIOSITY, CREATIVITY, COURAGE AND PASSION

What Lights Your Fire?

Your Unattended Longings

SPIRIT NOURISHMENT: EXPANDING, EXPLORING, LEARNING, AND GROWING

Ritual

Conclusion

Wow! Hooray! Yay!

You've made it! Celebrate yourself!

You've taken the time to learn and practice new happiness skills for your life. How are you doing? What do you notice that's new for you now? What's different in how you feel? What do you like the best about what you've learned? Go ahead; journal those answers. :)

Now keep going! Some of these skills have already become habits, which is wonderful. There are others that you are working on, and you know how to do this. You use your timer, put things in your planner, breathe, pause, and do the reset. You put up Post-it Notes and process through things in your journal. You continue to do all the right things to take impeccable care of your happiness and yourself.

Keep going. Set up accountability by doing this with a friend or connect with the Happiness Is a Skill group on Facebook. Hug yourself, celebrate yourself every day, and live the life that comes from loving you.

You're awesome!
Thank you for doing this work with me :)

Jane

If you want one-on-one coaching, contact me directly at
jane@happiness-is-a-skill.com

If you'd like to receive email updates about upcoming events, opt in
for the email list at http://happiness-is-a-skill.com

Let's Keep the Happiness Going

Jane Schreiner is a certified life and happiness coach who works with clients one-on-one. She is also a happiness speaker and teaches workshops, both in person and online. Visit www.happiness-is-a-skill.com for information on how to learn and practice happiness skills with Jane.

You can also join Jane at Facebook and Instagram:

 Say Yes to Happiness Handbook

 lifecoachjane

The Facebook page and Instagram are your places to find community and conversation with other people looking to grow their happiness too. Connection is a happiness skill, so let's stay connected!

Notes

Notes

Say YES to Happiness

Notes

Notes

Say YES to Happiness

Made in the USA
Coppell, TX
19 September 2022

83374306R00133